THE WHOLE FOOD PANTRY

ILLUSTRATED ENCYCLOPEDIA

THE
WHOLE FOOD
PANTRY

NICOLA GRAIMES

LORENZ BOOKS

This edition published in 2000 by Lorenz Books

LORENZ BOOKS are available for bulk purchase for sales promotion
and for premium use. For details, write or call the sales director,
Lorenz Books, 27 West 20th Street, New York, NY 10011;
(800) 354-9657

Lorenz Books is an imprint of Anness Publishing Inc.

Publisher: Joanna Lorenz
Executive Editor: Linda Fraser
Editor: Mariano Kalfors
Designer: Nigel Partridge
Photographer: Amanda Heywood
Home Economists: Kate Jay and Annabel Ford
Production Controller: Don Campaniello

Also published as *A Cook's Guide to Healthy Whole Foods* and, as part of a larger compendium, *The Practical Encyclopedia of Whole Foods*

Printed and bound in China
1 3 5 7 9 10 8 6 4 2

NOTES
Medium eggs are used unless otherwise stated
Use organically produced ingredients whenever possible, and always
choose unrefined flours and sugars, free-range eggs and live yoghurt

CONTENTS

Introduction

Throughout history, every culture has used food to prevent and treat illness and disease, and promote good health. The Egyptians praised the lentil for its ability to enlighten the mind; the Ancient Greeks and Romans used honey to heal wounds; while in China, sprouted beans and grains were used to treat a wide range of illnesses, from constipation to dropsy.

However, around the time of the industrial revolution, people in Western countries came to disregard the medicinal and therapeutic properties of food, and it is only relatively recently that interest in the healing qualities of food has been revived. This renewed interest, owing to our growing concern about what we eat and drink, and our quest for good health, is spurred on by scientists who have undertaken extensive research into eating habits, and have also investigated the properties of individual foods.

Numerous studies have revealed the positive attributes of a diet that is rich in fruit and vegetables, whole grains, nuts and seeds, and beans, complemented by a moderate amount of dairy foods. Studies have shown that vegetarians suffer less from diseases, such as obesity, cancer, heart disease, gallstones, diabetes, and constipation, that plague modern Western cultures. In fact, every scientific study comparing vegetarians with people eating a typical Western diet has found the former to be healthier and less likely to suffer from illness. Yet, vegetarianism is not just about achieving optimum health, it should also be an enjoyable and delicious way of eating.

WHAT ARE WHOLE FOODS?

Whole foods are foods to which nothing has been added or taken away. They are foods that haven't been unnecessarily processed or subjected to chemical processing, or loaded with harmful additives, colorings, or flavorings. In the narrowest sense, whole foods are specifically unrefined dried ingredients, such as grains, pulses, beans, and seeds, but in this book we have taken the liberty to expand the term to include all foods that should be included in a healthy diet. It is important to choose unrefined foods whenever you can, simply because they ensure the greatest intake of vitamins, minerals, and fiber. When food is processed, precious nutrients are taken away as a result, although there are various degrees to which this occurs. However, some would argue that a diet consisting entirely of whole foods could be decidedly brown and boring. A healthy whole foods diet should include a wide range of other ingredients to add both

Right: There is a wide range of organic produce available from health-food stores.

variety and essential nutrients. Plenty of fruit and vegetables, dairy products, fats and oils, and natural sweeteners are all needed to make whole foods palatable and appealing. And there's no reason why, if you are eating mainly whole foods, that you can't include a few refined foods. A little white flour added to a whole wheat cake or pastry, for instance, will give a much lighter end result and will affect only marginally the nutritional value. It is not such a sin to eat white rice instead of brown, or plain pasta rather than whole wheat occasionally, if the rest of the

Vegetarian Children

Children can thrive on a vegetarian diet as long as it is varied and balanced, and not based on foods such as chips and baked beans. Unlike adults, young children do not entirely benefit from a high-fiber, low-fat diet. They need plenty of calories and nutrients and, because they have small stomachs, require regular, small nutritious meals.

A diet based on low-fat and high-fiber foods can leads to malnutrition in young children because it does not provide sufficient nutrients and calories for growth and development. Reduced fat foods, such as skim milk and reduced-fat cheeses, lack much-needed calories, and their full-fat equivalents should be given to children under 2 years of age. High-fiber foods, such as brown rice, whole wheat bread and pasta, are too bulky for young children, and they become full before they have eaten enough nutrients. White bread and rice, and ordinary pasta are acceptable alternatives, provided they are eating plenty of fruit and vegetables, potatoes, cereals, beans, and lentils.

Children should avoid fizzy, caffeine- and sugar-laden drinks, and drink only small amounts of juices and squashes that contain artificial sweeteners, which can cause diarrhea if consumed in excess. Children should, instead, be encouraged to drink water, milk, and diluted fruit juice.

Above: Try to eat at least three portions of fruits and vegetables a day.

dish or meal is full of nutrient-packed, high-fiber foods.

It may be a cliché, but there is more than a grain of truth in the adage, "you are what you eat." Our bodies rely and thrive on a varied nutritious diet. Yet a healthy diet is not just about boosting physical welfare. Our mental and emotional wellbeing is equally affected by what we put on our plates. The more appetizing and appealing, the better.

ORGANIC FOODS

As food scares continue, many people are increasingly concerned about the type of food that they eat. The growing use of antibiotics, artificial additives, and chemicals as well as the introduction of irradiation and genetically-modified foods has added fuel to this concern. In 1995, 46 percent of fruits and vegetables analyzed in a UK study contained pesticide residues. A group of pesticides known as organophosphates have been a particular problem in carrots, while the results for celery are also disturbing.

People are looking for healthier, less processed foods, and the demand for organic foods is growing at a rate of about 30 percent every year. Organic foods were, until relatively recently, found only in health-food stores, but now there is an expanding range of fresh and packaged organic foods available from supermarkets. Reassuringly, every food that is labeled organic has to fulfill certain strict criteria. No artificial pesticides, fertilizers, or other chemicals can be used in the growing and/or production of organic food, and genetically-modified or irradiated ingredients are not permitted.

Traditional methods of agriculture, such as crop rotation, are used along with natural fertilizers. This preserves wildlife and minimizes pollution. Owing to their shorter shelf-life organic fruits and vegetables are less likely to have traveled thousands of miles before reaching stores. This could mean that in the future there may be a return to locally produced, seasonal foods. Whether organic food tastes better or is higher in nutrients is open to debate, but the environment and our health will undoubtedly benefit in the long-term.

The Essentials for Good Health

Along with water, there are six essential components for good health, which if consumed in the correct proportions, will provide the body with both sustained energy and the correct balance of nutrients required.

Below: Soluble fiber found in oats helps reduce blood cholesterol.

Carbohydrates

At one time, carbohydrates, which are made up of starches, fiber, and sugars, were considered to be fattening and less valuable than protein-rich foods. However, they are now recognized as the body's major source of energy and carbohydrate-rich foods supply a substantial amount of protein, vitamins, minerals, and fiber, with very little fat. About half the food we eat should be unrefined complex carbohydrates, such as whole-grain cereals, whole wheat bread and pasta, and brown rice. These high-fiber foods are broken down slowly

Below: Rice is a good source of insoluble fiber.

Fiber

Fruits, vegetables, grains, legumes, nuts, and seeds are our main source of fiber, of which there are two types: insoluble and soluble. Insoluble fiber, which is found in whole wheat, brown rice, bran, and nuts, provides bulk to the diet and helps to combat constipation. Soluble fiber, found in legumes, vegetables, and oats, binds with toxins in the gut and promotes their

by the body and provide a steady supply of energy. They are preferable to sugars or simple carbohydrates because these foods are quickly absorbed into the bloodstream and give only a short-term energy boost. When feasible, opt for unrefined carbohydrates, as the refined versions, such as white flour, rice, and sugar are stripped of nutrients, including vitamins, minerals, and fiber. It's important to remember that the more carbohydrates that you eat, the more you depend on them for supplying essential nutrients.

Right: Carbohydrate-rich vegetables, such as plantains, yams, and potatoes, provide a steady supply of energy.

excretion, and also helps to reduce blood cholesterol. Both types of fiber reduce the risk of bowel disorders, including diverticulitis, colon and rectal cancer, and irritable bowel syndrome (although bran has been found to aggravate symptoms of IBS). Few people get enough fiber. On average we eat about 12 grams of fiber a day, but we should be consuming about 18 grams. People who wish to lose weight will find that a high-fiber diet is beneficial, as it provides bulk and naturally limits the amount of food eaten.

Protein

This macro-nutrient is essential for the maintenance and repair of every cell in the body, and also ensures that enzymes, hormones, and antibodies function properly. Protein is made up of amino acids of which there are 20, and eight of these need to be supplied by diet. A food containing all eight amino acids is known as a "complete" or high-quality protein.

How to Increase Your Fiber Intake

• Base your diet on whole wheat bread and pasta, brown rice, and fruit and vegetables. Refined and processed foods contain less fiber and nutrients.
• Start the day with a whole-grain cereal, such as oatmeal or bran flakes.
• Eat plenty of dried fruit—add it to breakfast cereals, plain yogurt or use to make a compote.
• Add beans and lentils to salads and soups to boost their fiber content.
• Avoid peeling fruits and vegetables, if possible, as the skins contain valuable fiber.

Above: Nuts contain fat as well as protein.

For vegetarians, these include eggs and dairy products, as well as soybeans. Protein from plant sources, such as nuts, pasta, potatoes, legumes, cereals, and rice, do not usually contain all eight amino acids and are known as "incomplete" or low-quality protein. We should aim to get 10–15 percent of our calories from protein.

Vegetarians are often asked where they get their protein, and lack of this nutrient can be a concern for those cutting out meat and fish from their diet. Yet in reality,

Below: Buckwheat pasta is a "complete" protein.

most people eat too much protein and deficiency is virtually unheard of. In fact, an excess of protein can be detrimental, rather than beneficial to health. High-protein foods, such as dairy products and nuts, are a source of fat, and have been found to leach calcium from the body, which increases the risk of osteoporosis. It is also a common misconception that vegetarians have meticulously to combine protein foods in every meal to achieve the correct balance of amino acids. Nutritionists now believe that, provided a varied diet of grains, legumes, dairy produce, eggs, and vegetables is eaten on a daily basis, intentionally combining proteins is unnecessary.

Fats

A small amount of fat in the diet is essential for health. Fat not only provides vitamins A, D, and E and essential fatty acids that cannot be made in the body, but also contributes greatly to the taste, texture, and palatability of food. It contains a high number of calories, and should make up no more than 30 percent of your diet. The type of fat is as crucial as the quantity.

Saturated fat (found mainly in dairy products in the vegetarian diet) has been associated with an increased risk of cancer and coronary heart disease. Eating too much saturated fat can raise blood cholesterol levels and lead to narrowed arteries, more so than eating foods, such as eggs, that are high in cholesterol.

Left: Canola oil, which like olive and sesame oils is a monounsaturated fat and can help to reduce the levels of cholesterol in the body, also contains Omega-3 or linolenic acid, which is thought to reduce the risk of heart disease.

Unsaturated fats, both polyunsaturated and monounsaturated, can help to reduce harmful "LDL" cholesterol (the type that clogs up arteries) and, importantly, increase the beneficial "HDL" cholesterol, which is thought to reduce cholesterol levels in the body. Mono-unsaturated fats, such as olive oil, sesame oil, and canola oil, are less vulnerable to oxidation than polyunsaturated fats. Polyunsaturated fats provide essential fatty acids, omega-3 and 6. Omega-3 (linolenic acid), which is found in walnuts, soybeans, wheatgerm, and canola oil, has been found to reduce the risk of heart disease, while omega-6 (linoleic acid), which is found in nuts, seeds, and oils is thought to reduce levels of blood cholesterol.

Below: Parmesan cheese has a strong flavor, so it can be used in moderation.

How to Reduce Dietary Fat

While a vegetarian diet is often lower in fat than one based on meat, it is very easy to eat too many dairy products, oil-laden salad dressings and sauces, and high-fat ready-meals. Here are a few simple ways to reduce fat in your diet:

• Use strong, aged cheese, such as Parmesan—only a small amount is needed to add flavor to a dish

• Try making low-fat salad dressings using miso, orange juice, yogurt, herbs, spices, or tomato juice in place of oils

• Stir-fry foods using only a little oil. For best results make sure the wok/skillet is very hot before adding the oil

• Avoid blended oils, as they can contain coconut or palm oil which are both saturated fats

• Opt for low-fat cheeses, such as cottage, ricotta or mozzarella instead of high-fat cheeses, such as Cheddar

• Use low-fat yogurt instead of cream in cooked recipes. Stir in a spoonful of cornstarch (mixed to a paste with a little water) to prevent the yogurt curdling when heated

• Choose complex carbohydrates, including potatoes, pasta, brown rice, and beans, in preference to high-fat protein foods

Above: Use naturally low-fat cheeses, such as cottage cheese, ricotta and farmer's cheese.

Water

The importance of water is often taken for granted, yet although it is possible to survive for weeks without food, we can live for only a few days without water. Water plays a vital role in the body: it transports nutrients, regulates the body temperature, transports waste via the kidneys, and acts as a lubricating fluid. Most people do not drink enough water: it is thought that an adult requires around 10 cups per day. A shortage of water can provoke headaches and loss of concentration. Fizzy drinks, tea, and coffee all act as diuretics and speed up the loss of water, which causes dehydration.

Above: Eggs contain all eight essential amino acids, and are a good source of vitamin B$_{12}$.

Vitamins and Minerals

These nutrients are vital for good health and the functioning of our bodies, and with a few exceptions must be supplied by diet. The levels our bodies require vary depending on health, lifestyle, and age. Contrary to popular belief, vitamins and minerals do not provide energy, but assist in the release of energy provided by carbohydrates, fat, and protein.

Below: Oranges are rich in vitamin C.

How to Preserve Nutrients

The nutrients in food, particularly fruits and vegetables, are unstable and are diminished by time, preparation methods, and cooking. Leave a piece of cut fruit or a sliced potato exposed to air or soaking in water and its vitamin and mineral levels plummet. Old, wilted, or damaged produce also have reduced levels of vitamins and minerals. The following tips will ensure you get the most from your fruit and vegetables:

• Buy fruits and vegetables that are as fresh as possible and avoid those that have been stored under fluorescent light, as this can set off a chemical reaction that depletes nutrients.

• Buy loose fresh produce, which is much easier to check for quality than pre-packed foods.

• Buy fruit and vegetables in small quantities and do not keep them for too long, and remove them from plastic bags as soon as possible.

• Depending on the type of fruit or vegetable, store in a cool pantry or in the bottom of the refrigerator.

• Avoid peeling fruits and vegetables, if possible, and do not prepare them too far in advance of cooking, as nutrients such as vitamin C will be destroyed.

• Eat fruits and vegetables raw, when they are at their most nutritious.

• Avoid boiling vegetables because this method of cooking destroys water-soluble vitamins, such as thiamine and vitamins B and C. If you must boil vegetables, use as little water as possible and do not overcook them. The cooking water can also be kept and used as stock for soup.

It is not just fruit and vegetables that benefit from careful storage and handling—nuts, seeds, legumes, and grains will also be fresher and have a higher nutrient content if stored and cooked correctly.

Right: Miso contains a good amount of the water-soluble vitamin B$_{12}$.

Vitamins are either water-soluble or fat-soluble. Fat-soluble vitamins A, D, E, and K are stored in the liver for some time. Water-soluble vitamins, B complex and C, cannot be stored and must be replaced on a daily basis. If you drink alcohol or smoke, increase your intake of vitamin B- and C-rich foods. Of the B-complex vitamins, vegetarians should make sure they get enough B$_{12}$, although this shouldn't be difficult as it is

required only in tiny amounts. It is found in dairy products, fortified breakfast cereals, yeast extract, miso, and eggs.

There are 16 essential minerals; some like calcium, are required in relatively large amounts, while trace elements, such as selenium and magnesium, are needed in tiny quantities. Minerals have various functions, but predominantly regulate and balance the body and maintain a healthy immune system. A deficiency of iron affects one-fifth of the world's population, and vegetarians need to make a point of eating iron-rich foods.

Essential Vitamins and Minerals

VITAMIN	BEST VEGETARIAN SOURCES	ROLE IN HEALTH	DEFICIENCY
A (retinol in animal foods, beta carotene in plant foods)	*animal sources:* milk, butter, cheese, egg yolks, and margarine *plant sources:* carrots, apricots, squash, red bell peppers, broccoli, leafy greens, mango, and sweet potatoes	Essential for vision, bone growth, and skin and tissue repair. Beta carotene acts as an antioxidant and protects the immune system	Deficiency is characterized by poor night vision, dry skin, and lower resistance to infection, especially respiratory disorders
B_1 (thiamin)	Wholegrain cereals, brewer's yeast, potatoes, nuts, pulses, and milk	Essential for energy production, the nervous system, muscles, and heart. Promotes growth and boosts mental ability	Deficiency is characterized by depression, irritability, nervous disorders, loss of memory. Common among alcoholics
B_2 (riboflavin)	Cheese, eggs, milk, yogurt, fortified breakfast cereals, yeast extract, almonds, and pumpkin seeds	Essential for energy production and for the functioning of vitamin B6 and niacin, as well as tissue repair.	Deficiency is characterized by lack of energy, dry cracked lips, numbness, and itchy eyes
Niacin (part of B complex)	Pulses, potatoes, fortified breakfast cereals, wheatgerm, peanuts, milk, cheese, eggs, peas, mushrooms, leafy greens, figs, and prunes	Essential for healthy digestive system, skin, and circulation. It is also needed for the release of energy	Deficiency is unusual, but characterized by lack of energy, depression, and scaly skin
B_6 (piridoxine)	Eggs, whole wheat bread, breakfast cereals, nuts, bananas, and cruciferous vegetables, such as broccoli, cabbage, and cauliflower	Essential for assimilating protein and fat, to make red blood cells, and a healthy immune system	Deficiency is characterized by anemia, dermatitis, and depression
B_{12} (cyanocobalamin)	Milk, eggs, fortified breakfast cereals, cheese, and yeast extract	Essential for formation of red blood cells, maintaining a healthy nervous system, and increasing energy levels	Deficiency is characterized by fatigue, increase risk of infection, anemia
Folate (folic acid)	Leafy greens, fortified breakfast cereals, bread, nuts, pulses, bananas, and yeast extract	Essential for cell division; makes genetic material (DNA) for every cell. Extra is needed pre-conception and during pregnancy to protect fetus against neural tube defects	Deficiency characterized by anemia and appetite loss. Linked with neural defects in babies
C (ascorbic acid)	Citrus fruit, melons, strawberries, tomatoes, broccoli, potatoes, bell peppers, and green vegetables	Essential for the absorption of iron, healthy skin, teeth, and bones. An antioxidant that strengthens the immune system and helps fight infection	Deficiency characterized by increased susceptibility to infection, fatigue, poor sleep, and depression
D (calciferol)	Sunlight, margarine, vegetable oils, eggs, cereals, and butter	Essential for bone and teeth formation, helps the body to absorb calcium and phosphorus	Deficiency characterized by softening of the bones, muscle weakness, and anemia. Long-term shortage in children results in rickets
E (tocopherol)	Seeds, nuts, vegetable oils, eggs, whole wheat bread, leafy greens, oats, and cereals	Essential for healthy skin, circulation, and maintaining cells—an antioxidant	Deficiency characterized by increased risk of heart attack, strokes, and certain cancers

MINERAL	BEST VEGETARIAN SOURCES	ROLE IN HEALTH	DEFICIENCY
Calcium	Milk, cheese, yogurt, leafy greens, sesame seeds, broccoli, dried figs, pulses, almonds, spinach, and watercress	Essential for building and maintaining bones and teeth, muscle function, and the nervous system	Deficiency characterized by soft and brittle bones, osteoporosis, fractures, and muscle weakness
Iron	Egg yolks, fortified breakfast cereals, leafy greens, dried apricots, prunes, pulses, whole grains, and bean curd	Essential for healthy blood and muscles	Deficiency characterized by anemia, fatigue, and low resistance to infection.
Zinc	Peanuts, cheese, whole grains, sunflower and pumpkin seeds, pulses, milk, hard cheese, and yogurt	Essential for a healthy immune system, tissue formation, normal growth, wound healing, and reproduction	Deficiency is characterized by impaired growth and development, slow wound healing, and loss of taste and smell
Sodium	Most salt we eat comes from processed foods, such as chips, cheese, and canned foods. It is also found naturally in most foods.	Essential for nerve and muscle function and the regulation of body fluid	Deficiency is unlikely but can lead to dehydration, cramps, and muscle weakness.
Potassium	Bananas, milk, pulses, nuts, seeds, whole grains, potatoes, fruits, and vegetables	Essential for water balance, normal blood pressure, and nerve transmission	Deficiency is characterized by weakness, thirst, fatigue, mental confusion, and raised blood pressure
Magnesium	Nuts, seeds, whole grains, pulses, bean curd, dried figs and apricots, and green vegetables	Essential for healthy muscles, bones and teeth, normal growth, and nerves	Deficiency is characterized by lethargy, weak bones and muscles, depression, and irritability.
Phosphorus	Milk, cheese, yogurt, eggs, nuts, seeds, pulses, and whole grains	Essential for healthy bones and teeth, energy production, and the assimilation of nutrients, particularly calcium	Deficiency is rare
Selenium	Avocados, lentils, milk, cheese, butter, Brazil nuts, and seaweed	Essential for protecting against free radical damage and may protect against cancer—an antioxidant	Deficiency is characterized by reduced antioxidant protection
Iodine	Seaweed and iodized salt	Aids the production of hormones released by the thyroid gland	Deficiency can lead to the formation of a goiter and a sluggish metabolism and apathy, as well as dry skin and hair
Chloride	Table salt and foods that contain table salt	Regulates and maintains the balance of fluids in the body	Deficiency is rare
Manganese	Nuts, whole grains, pulses, bean curd, and tea	Essential component of various enzymes that are involved in energy production	Deficiency is not characterized by any specific symptoms

The Whole Food Kitchen

This fascinating guide includes every kind of natural food, from fruit and vegetables to grains, and from dairy foods to herbs and spices. It includes essential facts about key health benefits and traditional healing qualities, as well as information on buying and storing, preparing and cooking whole foods. It is an inspiration to anyone interested in finding out more about foods that can make you live, look, and feel better.

Fruit

Perhaps the ultimate convenience food, most fruits can be simply washed and eaten and, because the nutrients are concentrated just below the skin, it is best to avoid peeling. Cooking fruit reduces valuable vitamins and minerals, so, if you can, eat it raw. Fruit is an excellent source of energy and provides valuable fiber and antioxidants, which are said to reduce the risk of heart disease and certain cancers. Thanks to modern farming methods and efficient transportation, most fruit is available all year round, although it is generally best when homegrown, organically produced, and in season.

Orchard Fruits

These fruits have a long history, spanning thousands of years, and offer an incredible range of colors and flavors. This group includes many favorites, from crisp, juicy apples, which are available all year round, to luscious, fragrant peaches—a popular summer fruit.

APPLES

There are thousands of varieties of apple, although the choice in stores is often restricted to a mere few. Some of the most popular eating varieties are Empire, Winesap McIntosh, Granny Smith, Gala, Braeburn, and Golden and Red Delicious.

The Bramley Seedling, with its thick, shiny, green skin and tart flesh, is the most familiar cooking apple and is perfect for baking, or as the basis of apple sauce. Some lesser-known varieties, many of which have a short season, are often available from farm stores. Homegrown apples bought out of season may have spent several months in cold storage, where ripening and maturation are artificially halted. When they are taken out of storage, the apples deteriorate quickly.

Apples are delicious when they are eaten raw with their

Apricots

skin on. However, this versatile fruit is often used in breakfast dishes, main meals, salads, desserts, pies, and even soups. Large cooking apples are ideal puréed, stewed, and baked, but their tartness means that sugar has to be added. Some varieties of eating apple are just as good cooked and don't need any added sugar.

To preserve the maximum amount of vitamins and minerals, cook apples over low heat with little or no water. Most of the insecticides that are used on apples collect in the apple core and seeds, so, unless the apples are organic, these should be removed before cooking.

Buying and Storing: When buying apples, choose bright, firm fruits without any bruises. Organic apples are

An Apple a Day

Numerous studies have shown that eating apples regularly could reduce harmful LDL cholesterol in the body. In France, 30 middle-aged men and women were asked to add 2–3 apples a day to their diet for a month. By the end of the month, 80 percent of the group showed reduced cholesterol levels, and in half of the group the drop was more than 10 percent. Additionally, the level of good HDL cholesterol went up. Pectin, a soluble fiber found particularly in apples, is believed to be the magic ingredient.

Large cooking apples (left) and eating apples

Baked Apples

Baking is a simple and nutritious way of cooking this orchard fruit. Use large apples, such as Greening.

1 Preheat the oven to 350°F. Remove the cores of the apples, then score the skin around the circumference of each to prevent the skin bursting. Place the apples in an ovenproof dish with a little water.

2 Fill the cavity of the apples with a mixture of dark brown sugar, dried fruit, and nuts. Top each with a pat of butter and bake for about 40 minutes, or until the apples are soft.

more prone to blemishes than non-organic ones, and the fruits can look a little tatty, but the taste will often be superior. Smaller apples tend to have a better flavor and texture than larger specimens. Store apples in a cool place, away from direct sunlight.

Health Benefits: The cleansing and blood-purifying qualities of apples are highly valued in natural medicine. Apples aid digestion and can remove impurities in the liver. They are a good source of vitamin C and fiber, if you eat the skin. Although low in calories, they contain fructose, a simple sugar that is released slowly to supply the body with energy and balance blood-sugar levels. People with skin problems and arthritis are said to benefit from eating apples regularly.

APRICOTS

The best apricots are sunshine gold in color and full of juice. They are delicious baked or used raw in salads.

Buying and Storing: An apricot is at its best when truly ripe. Immature fruits are hard and tasteless and never seem to attain the right level of sweetness.

Health Benefits: Extremely rich in beta carotene, minerals, and vitamin A, apricots are a valuable source of fiber.

CHERRIES

There are two types: sweet and sour. Some are best eaten raw, like the popular Bing, while others, such as Morello, are best cooked.

Buying and Storing: Choose firm, bright, glossy fruits that have fresh, green stems. Discard any that are soft or have split or damaged skin.

Glossy, red, sweet cherries

Health Benefits: Cherries stimulate and cleanse the system, removing toxins from the kidneys. They are a remedy for gout and arthritis. Cherries also contain iron, potassium, vitamins C and B, as well as beta carotene.

NECTARINES

Like a peach without the fuzzy skin, this sweet juicy fruit is named after the drink of the gods—nectar—and is delicious baked or used raw in salads.

Buying and Storing: see Peaches.

Health Benefits: When eaten raw, nectarines are especially rich in vitamin C. They aid the digestion, effectively reduce high blood pressure, and cleanse the body.

PEACHES

These summer fruits are prized for their perfume and luscious juiciness. Peaches range in color from gold to deep red, and the flesh can be orange or white.

Buying and Storing: Avoid overly soft fruit. Peaches and nectarines are extremely fragile and bruise easily, so buy when

Nectarines and peaches

slightly under-ripe. To ripen them quickly, place in a brown paper bag with an already ripened fruit. Store ripe nectarines and peaches in the fridge, but bring back to room temperature before eating.

Health Benefits: Much of the vitamin C content of a peach lies in and just under its delicate skin, so eat the fruit unpeeled. Peaches are an excellent source of the antioxidant beta carotene, which is said to lower the risk of heart disease and some forms of cancer.

PEARS

Pears have been popular for thousands of years and were extensively cultivated by both the Greeks and the Romans. Pears come into their own in the late summer and fall with the arrival of the new season's crops. Particular favorites are green and brown-skinned Conference; Williams, with its thin, yellow skin and sweet, soft flesh;

plump Comice, which has a pale yellow skin with a green tinge; and Packham, an excellent cooking pear.

Like certain apples, some types of pear are good for cooking, others are best eaten raw, and a few varieties fit happily into both camps.

Pears can be used in both sweet and non-sweet dishes; they are excellent in salads, and can be baked, poached in syrup, and used in pies. Pears are unlikely to cause any allergic reactions, so when cooked and puréed they make perfect food for weaning babies.

Buying and Storing: Choose firm, plump fruit that are just slightly under-ripe. Pears can ripen in a day or so and then they pass their peak very quickly, and become woolly or mushy. To tell if a pear is ripe, feel around the base of the stalk, where it should give slightly when gently pressed, but the pear itself should be firm.

Health Benefits: Despite their high water content, pears contain useful amounts of vitamin C, fiber, and potassium. In natural medicine, they are used as a diuretic and laxative. Rich in pectin and soluble fiber, pears could also be valuable in lowering harmful cholesterol levels in the body. Eating pears regularly is said to result in a clear, healthy complexion and glossy hair.

PLUMS

Ranging in color from pale yellow to dark, rich purple, plums come in many different varieties, although only a few are available in stores. They can be sweet and juicy or slightly tart; the latter are best cooked in pies and cakes, or made into a delicious jelly. Sweet plums can be eaten as they are, and are good in fruit salads, or they can be puréed and combined with custard or yogurt to make a fruit fool.

*From left, Conference,
Comice, and Williams pears*

Plums

QUINCE

Fragrant, with a thin, yellow or green skin, these knobby fruits, which can be either apple- or pear-shaped, are always cooked. Their high pectin content means that they are good for jellies and, in Spain and France, quinces are used to make a fruit paste that is served with soft cheeses.

Buying and Storing: Look for smooth ripe fruits that are not too soft. Quinces keep well and can be stored in a bowl in your kitchen or living room. They will fill the room with their delicious scent.

Health Benefits: Quinces are rich in soluble fiber and pectin. They also calm the stomach and allay nausea.

Plums should be just firm, and not too soft, with shiny, smooth skin that has a slight "bloom." Store ripe plums in the fridge. Unripe fruits can be kept at room temperature for a few days to ripen. Plums relieve constipation and are thought to stimulate the nerves.

Yellow, pear-shaped quince

Dried Fruit

A useful source of energy, dried fruit is higher in calories than fresh fruit, and packed with vitamins and minerals. The drying process boosts the levels of vitamin C, beta carotene, potassium, and iron. Apricots and prunes are the most popular types, but dried apple rings, cherries, and peaches are also available. Sulfur, often used as a preservative in dried fruits, is best avoided, especially by people who suffer from asthma. Look for unsulfured fruit.

Pitting Fruit

1 To remove the pits from peaches, apricots, or plums, cut around the middle of the fruit down to the pit with a paring knife. Twist each half of the fruit in opposite directions.

2 Prize out the pit using the tip of the knife and discard. Rub the cut flesh with lemon juice.

Citrus Fruits

Juicy and brightly colored, citrus fruits, such as oranges, grapefruit, lemons, and limes are best known for their sweet, slightly sour juice, which is rich in vitamin C. They are invaluable in the kitchen, adding an aromatic acidity to many dishes, from soups and sauces to desserts and pies. Buy organic fruit when you can, and eat within a week or two.

ORANGES

Best eaten as soon as they are peeled, oranges start to lose vitamin C from the moment they are cut. Thin-skinned oranges tend to be the juiciest.

Popular varieties include the Navel (named after the belly button-type spot at the flower end), which contains no pits and so is good for slicing; sweet, juicy Jaffa and Valencia; and Seville, a sour orange used to make marmalade.

The outermost layer of the orange rind can be removed using a swivel vegetable peeler or paring knife. This thin rind contains aromatic oils, which give a delightful perfumed flavor to both non-sweet and sweet dishes.

Oranges

GRAPEFRUIT

The flesh of the grapefruit ranges in color from vivid pink and ruby red to white; the pink and red varieties are sweeter. Heavier fruits are likely to be juicier. Served juiced, halved, or cut into slices, grapefruit can provide a refreshing start to the day. The fruit also adds a refreshing tang to salads or a contrast to rich foods. Cooking or broiling mellows the tartness, but keep cooking times brief to preserve the nutrients. A glass of grapefruit juice before bed is said to promote sleep.

LEMONS

Both the juice and rind of this essential cooking ingredient can be used to enliven salad dressings, vegetables, marinades, sauces, and cookies. Lemon juice can also be used to prevent some fruits and vegetables from discoloring when cut. Lemons should be deep yellow in color, firm and heavy for their size, with no hint of green in the skin, as this is a sign of immaturity, while a thin, smooth skin is a sign of juicy flesh. A slice of lemon in hot water cleanses the system and invigorates the whole body.

Citrus Nutrients

Eating an orange a day will generally supply an adult's requirement for vitamin C, but citrus fruits also contain phosphorus, potassium, calcium, beta carotene, and fiber. Pectin, a soluble fiber that is found in the flesh and particularly in the membranes of citrus fruit, has been shown to reduce cholesterol levels. The membranes also contain bioflavonoids, which have powerful antioxidant properties. Drink fresh fruit juice when you can, as bottled, canned, and concentrated citrus juices have reduced levels of vitamin C.

Grapefruit

Lemons

With a spoonful of honey added, a hot lemon drink is an old and trusted remedy for alleviating colds and flu.

LIMES

Once considered to be rather exotic, limes are now widely available. Avoid fruits with a yellowing skin, as this is a sign of deterioration. The juice has a sharper flavor than that of lemons and if you substitute limes for lemons in a recipe, you will need to use less juice. Limes are used a great deal in Asian cooking and the rind can be used to flavor curries, marinades, and dips. Cilantro, chile peppers, garlic, and ginger are natural partners.

The Powers of Vitamin C

Citrus fruit is best known for its generous vitamin C content, which is found predominantly in the flesh. An antioxidant, vitamin C has been found to thwart many forms of cancer (particularly cancer of the stomach and esophagus) by defending body cells against harmful free radicals. Free radicals attack DNA—the cell's genetic material—causing them to mutate and possibly become cancerous.

Numerous population studies have also demonstrated that a high dietary intake of vitamin C significantly reduces the risk of death from the world's greatest killers: the heart attack and stroke. It has been found both to lower harmful LDL cholesterol in the body and to raise beneficial HDL cholesterol. It does this by converting LDL cholesterol into bile acids, which are normally excreted. If vitamin C is in short supply, LDL cholesterol accumulates in the body.

The ability of vitamin C to boost the immune system by helping to fight viruses is well documented. It can be particularly beneficial for infections of the urinary tract and the herpes simplex virus. Researchers are in two minds as to whether vitamin C actually prevents colds, but they certainly agree that it can lessen the severity and length of colds and flu. It also boosts the body's ability to absorb iron from food.

Vitamin C is destroyed by heat as well as being water soluble, and is therefore easily lost in cooking. If fruits are cut some time before eating, much of their vitamin C content will also be lost.

Limes are a good source of vitamin C.

Grating Citrus Rind

1 To remove long, thin shreds of rind, use a zester. Scrape it along the surface of the fruit, applying firm pressure.

2 For finer shreds, use a grater. Rub the fruit over the fine cutters to remove the rind without any of the white pith.

Cutting Fine Strips or Julienne

1 Using a vegetable peeler, remove strips of orange rind making sure the white pith is left behind on the fruit.

2 Stack several strips of citrus rind and, using a sharp knife, cut them into fine strips or julienne.

Buying and Storing: Look for plump, firm citrus fruit that feels heavy for its size, and has a smooth thin skin; this indicates that the flesh is juicy. Fruits with bruises, brown spots, green patches (or yellow patches on limes), and soft, mushy skin should be avoided, as should dry, wrinkled specimens. Citrus fruits can be kept at room temperature for a few days but if you want to keep them longer, they are best stored in the fridge and eaten within two weeks. Most citrus fruits are waxed or sprayed with fungicides, so scrub them thoroughly to remove any residues. If you can, buy organic or unwaxed fruit.

COOK'S TIPS

• *Rolling citrus fruit firmly over a work surface or in the palms of your hands will help you extract the maximum amount of juice from the fruit.*

• *Limes and lemons will yield more juice if cut lengthwise, rather than horizontally.*

Berries and Currants

These baubles of vivid red, purple, and black are the epitome of summer and fall, although they are now likely to be found all year round. Despite their distinctive appearance and flavor, berries and currants are interchangeable in their uses—jellies and pies are the obvious choices. Interestingly, they also share health-giving qualities, including the ability to treat stomach problems and cleanse the blood, and therefore play a part in natural medicine.

STRAWBERRIES

These are the favorite summer fruits and do not need any embellishment. Serve ripe (avoid those with white or green tips) and raw, on their own, or with a little cream or some natural yogurt. Wash only if absolutely necessary and just before serving.

Strawberries

Health Benefits: Strawberries are rich in B complex vitamins and vitamin C. They contain significant amounts of potassium, and have good skin-cleansing properties.

RASPBERRIES

Soft and fragrant, raspberries are best served simply and unadulterated—maybe with a spoonful of natural yogurt. Those grown in Scotland are regarded as the best in the world. Raspberries are very fragile and require the minimum of handling, so wash only if really necessary. They are best eaten raw, as cooking spoils their flavor and vitamin C content.

Raspberries

Health Benefits: Raspberries are a rich source of vitamin C. They are effective in treating menstrual cramps, as well as cleansing the body, and removing toxins. Raspberry leaf tea is often drunk in the last few weeks of pregnancy, as it prepares the uterus for labor.

Cranberry Cure

A recent study reported in the Journal of the American Medical Research Association supports the long-held belief that cranberries combat cystitis and other infections of the urinary tract. It found that drinking cranberry juice reduces levels of bacteria not only in the urinary tract, but also in the bladder and kidneys.

BLUEBERRIES

Dark purple in color, blueberries are very popular in the United States. When ripe, the berries are plump and slightly firm, with a natural "bloom." Avoid any that are soft and dull-skinned, and wash and dry carefully to avoid bruising. Cultivated blueberries are larger than wild ones. Both types are sweet enough to be eaten raw, but are also good cooked in pies and muffins, used for jellies, or made into a sauce to serve with nut or vegetable roasts. Unwashed blueberries will keep for up to a week in the bottom of the fridge.

Health Benefits: Numerous studies show that eating blueberries regularly can improve night vision as well as protect against the onset of cataracts and glaucoma. Blueberries are also effective in treating urinary tract infections and can improve poor circulation.

BLACKBERRIES

These are a familiar sight in early fall, growing wild in hedgerows. Cultivated blackberries have a slightly longer season and are generally much larger than the wild fruits. Juicy and plump, blackberries can vary in sweetness, which is why they are so often cooked. Wash them carefully to prevent bruising the fruits, then pat dry with paper towels. Use in pies, or make into jellies. The berries can also be lightly cooked, then puréed, and pressed through a strainer to make a sauce to serve with other fruits or ice cream. Blackberries make an ideal partner to apples and pears.

Blackberries

Blueberries

Health Benefits: Blackberries are high in fiber and contain a wealth of minerals, including magnesium, iron, and calcium. They are rich in vitamin C, and are one of the best low-fat sources of vitamin E. In natural medicine, blackberries are used to cleanse the blood and they have a tonic effect. They are also used to ease stomach complaints and to treat menstrual problems. Blackberries are particularly rich in bioflavonoids, which act as antioxidants, inhibiting the growth of cancer cells and protecting against cell damage by carcinogens.

GOOSEBERRIES

A favorite fruit of Northern Europe, gooseberries are relatively rare in other parts of the world. They range from the hard and sour green type to the sweeter, softer purple variety. The skin can vary from smooth and silky to fuzzy and spiky. Slightly unripe, tart gooseberries make wonderful pies, crumbles, and jellies. Ripe, softer fruits can be puréed and mixed with cream, yogurt, or custard to make a delicious fruit fool.

Health Benefits: Rich in vitamin C, gooseberries also contain beta carotene, potassium, and fiber.

Black currants

BLACK CURRANTS, RED CURRANTS AND WHITE CURRANTS

These pretty, delicate fruits are usually sold in bunches on the stem. To remove the currants from the stalk, run the prongs of a fork down through the clusters, taking care not to damage the fruit. Wash the fruits carefully, then pat dry. Raw black currants are quite tart, but this makes

White currants

them ideal for cooking in sweet pies. They make delicious jellies, and are especially good in a traditional summer pudding when they are partnered by other berries. Sweeter white currants make a delightful addition to fruit salads.

Health Benefits: The nutritional value of currants has long been recognized. They are high in antioxidants, vitamins C and E, and carotenes. They also contain significant amounts of fiber, calcium, iron, and magnesium. In natural medicine, black currants are often used to settle stomach upsets.

Red currants

Buying and Storing: Look for firm, glossy berries and currants. Make sure that they are not squashed or moldy. Ripe fruits generally do not keep well and are best eaten on the day of purchase—store in the fridge. Unripe fruits can be kept for longer. Raspberries, blueberries, blackberries, and currants all freeze well.

Gooseberries

Fruit Purée

Soft berries are perfect for making uncooked fruit purées or coulis. Sweeten if the fruit is tart and add a splash of lemon juice to bring out the flavor.

1 To make raspberry purée, process some raspberries, with lemon juice and confectioner's sugar to taste, in a food processor or blender until smooth.

2 Press through a nylon strainer. Store in the fridge for up to two days.

Grapes, Melons, Dates, and Figs

These fruits were some of the first ever to be cultivated and are therefore steeped in history. They are available in an immense variety of shapes, colors, and sizes, and with the exception of melons, they can also be bought dried. As well as being a good source of nutrients, these fruits are high in soluble fiber.

GRAPES

There are many varieties of grape, each with its own particular flavor and character. Most are grown for wine production. Grapes for eating are less acidic and have a thinner skin than those used for wine-making. Seedless grapes are easier to eat and contain less tannin than the seeded fruit. Grapes range in color from deep purple to pale red, and from bright green to almost white. The finest eating grapes are Muscat grapes, which have a wonderful, perfumed flavor. They may be pale

Red and green grapes

green or golden, or black or red. Italia grapes, another popular eating variety, have a luscious musky flavor and may be green or black. Unless they are organic, grapes should be thoroughly washed before eating as they are routinely sprayed with pesticides and fungicides.

Serve grapes with cheese, in salads, or as a topping for a pie. Before cooking them, remove the skin by blanching the grapes in boiling water for a few seconds, then peel with a small knife.

A Glass of Red Wine

According to a recent American study, phenolic is just one of the compounds found in red wine that may delay the onset of cancer. This news comes following research that wine—particularly red wine—may reduce the risk of heart disease. Nutritionally, wine is virtually worthless and should be drunk in moderation, although it may increase the absorption of iron if drunk with a meal.

Buying and Storing: Buy grapes that are plump, and fairly firm. They should be evenly colored and firmly attached to the stalk. Unwashed fruit may be stored in the fridge for up to five days.

Health Benefits: Grapes contain iron, potassium, and fiber. They are powerful detoxifiers and can improve the condition of the skin, and treat gout, liver, and kidney disorders. Research has revealed that resveratrol, a natural substance produced by grapes, can help inhibit the formation

Galia melons (front left and back), Cantaloupe melons (center), and watermelon (right)

of tumors and that purple grape juice may be even more effective than aspirin in reducing the risk of heart attacks.

MELONS

Watermelons are very low in calories because of their high water content, which is around 90 percent. They contain less vitamin C than the fragrant, orange-fleshed varieties, such as the Cantaloupe and Charentais. Avoid buying ready-cut melons, because most of the vitamins will have been lost.

Buying and Storing: Look for melons that feel heavy for their size and yield to gentle pressure at the stem end.

Health Benefits: When they are eaten on their own, melons are easy to digest and pass quickly through the system. But when they are consumed with other foods requiring a more complex digestive process, they may actually inhibit the absorption of nutrients.

Figs

FIGS

These delicate, thin-skinned fruits may be purple, brown, or greenish-gold. Delicious raw, figs can also be poached or baked. Choose unbruised, ripe fruits that yield to gentle pressure and eat on the day of purchase. If they are not too ripe, they can be kept in the fridge for a day or two. Figs are a well-known laxative and an excellent source of calcium.

DATES

Like figs, dates are one of the oldest cultivated fruits, possibly dating back as far as 50,000 BC. Fresh dates are sweet and soft and make a good natural sweetener: purée the cooked fruit, then add to cake or bread mixtures, or simply mix into natural yogurt to make a quick dessert. Dates should be plump and glossy. Medjool dates from Egypt and California have a wrinkly skin, but most other varieties are smooth. They can be stored in the fridge for up to a week. Dates are high in vitamin C and a good source of potassium and soluble fiber.

Fresh dates

Dried Vine Fruits

Currants, raisins, and golden raisins are the most popular dried fruits. Traditionally, these vine fruits are used for fruit cakes and breads, but currants and raisins are also good in non-sweet dishes. In Indian and North African cookery they are frequently used for their sweetness. Figs and dates are also popular—chopped or puréed—as an ingredient in cakes, fruit breads and pastries.

It takes about 4–5 pounds of fresh grapes to produce 1 pound of raisins or currants, while 3 pounds of fresh figs and dates produce just 1 pound of dried fruit. Although high in natural sugars, which can damage teeth if eaten to excess, dried fruit is a concentrated source of nutrients, including iron, potassium, calcium, phosphorus, vitamin C, beta carotene, and some B vitamins.

Tropical Fruit

This exotic collection of fruits ranges from the familiar bananas and pineapples to the more unusual papayas and passion fruit. The diversity in colors, shapes, and flavors is sure to excite the tastebuds.

PINEAPPLES

These distinctive-looking fruits have a sweet, exceedingly juicy, and golden flesh. Unlike most other fruits, pineapples do not ripen after picking, although leaving a slightly unripe fruit for a few days at room temperature may reduce its acidity.

Mangoes

Buying and Storing: Choose pineapples that have fresh green spiky leaves, are heavy for their size, and are slightly soft to the touch. Store in the fridge when ripe.

Health Benefits: Pineapple contains an antibacterial enzyme called bromelain, which has anti-inflammatory properties and should help arthritis sufferers. It also aids digestion.

PAPAYA

Also known as pawpaw, these pear-shaped fruits come from South America. When ripe, the green skin turns a speckled yellow, and the pulp is a glorious orange-pink color. The numerous edible, small black seeds taste peppery when dried. Peel off the skin using a sharp knife or a vegetable peeler before enjoying the creamy flesh, which has a lovely perfumed aroma and sweet flavor. Ripe papaya is best eaten raw, while unripe green fruit can be used in cooking.

Health Benefits: Papaya contains an enzyme called papain, which aids the digestion,

although levels of this enzyme diminish with ripening. Skin, hair, and nails all benefit from the generous amounts of vitamin C and beta carotene found in papaya. Iron, potassium, and calcium are also present.

MANGO

The skin of these luscious, fragrant fruits can range in color from green to yellow, orange, or red. Their shape varies tremendously, too. An entirely green skin is a sign of an unripe fruit, although in Asia, these are often used in salads. Ripe fruit should yield to gentle pressure and, when cut, it should reveal a juicy, orange flesh. Preparing a mango can be awkward (see opposite). Serve sliced, or purée and use as a base for ice creams and sorbets.

Health Benefits: Rich in vitamin C and beta carotene, mangoes are also reputed to cleanse the blood.

Other Tropical Fruit

Kiwi fruit, which is also known as the Chinese gooseberry, has a brown, downy skin and vivid green flesh that is peppered with tiny black seeds. It is extremely rich in vitamin C.

Passionfruit is a dark purple, wrinkly, egg-shaped fruit, which hides a pulpy, golden flesh with edible black seeds. Cut in half and scoop out the inside with a spoon. Passionfruit is rich in vitamins A and C.

Large and baby pineapples

Preparing Mango

Mangoes can be awkward to prepare because they have a large, flat pit that is slightly off-center. The method below produces cubed fruit. Alternatively, the mango can be peeled with a vegetable peeler and sliced around the central pit.

1 | Hold the fruit with one hand and cut vertically down one side of the pit. Repeat on the opposite side. Cut away any remaining flesh around the pit.

2 Taking the two large slices, and using a sharp knife, cut the flesh into a criss-cross pattern down to the skin. Holding the mango skin side down, press it inside out, then cut the mango cubes off from the skin.

COOK'S TIP

To ripen fruit, place it in a paper bag with an already ripened fruit and leave at room temperature or in a warm place.

Papaya

BANANAS

A concentrated bundle of energy, bananas are also full of valuable nutrients. The soft and creamy flesh can be blended into smooth, sweet drinks, mashed and mixed with yogurt, or the fruits can be baked and grilled whole. Bananas also make an ideal weaning food for babies, as they rarely cause an allergic reaction.

Health Benefits: Bananas are rich in dietary fiber, vitamins, and minerals, especially potassium, which is important for the functioning of cells, nerves, and muscles, and can relieve high blood pressure. Ripe bananas soothe the stomach and are believed to strengthen the stomach lining against acid and ulcers. Their high starch content makes them a good source of sustained energy, and they are also an effective laxative. Bananas are rich in the amino acid tryptophan, which is known to lift the spirits and aid sleep.

Buying and Storing: When buying, look for fruit that is heavy for its size. Mangoes and papayas should yield to gentle pressure. Avoid overly soft or bruised fruit, or those with any hard spots. Fully ripe mangoes and papayas are best kept in the fridge. If you wish to buy ripe bananas, choose yellow (or red) fruit that are patched with brown. Bananas with patches of green can be ripened at room temperature. Don't buy completely green bananas, as these rarely ripen properly. Store bananas at cool room temperature.

Sweet, red-skinned bananas and the more familiar large and small yellow-skinned varieties

Vegetables

Vegetables offer an infinite number of culinary possibilities to the cook. The choice is immense and the growing demand for organic produce has meant that pesticide-free vegetables are now increasingly available. Vegetables are an essential component of a healthy diet and have countless nutritional benefits. They are at their best when freshly picked.

Roots and Tubers

Vegetables such as carrots, rutabagas, parsnips and potatoes, are comforting and nourishing food, and it is not surprising that they should be popular in the winter. Their sweet, dense flesh provides sustained energy, valuable fiber, vitamins, and minerals.

Fresh carrots with their green, feathery tops

CARROTS

The best carrots are not restricted to the cold winter months. Summer welcomes the slender sweet new crop, often sold with their green, feathery tops. (These are best removed after buying, as they rob the root of moisture and nutrients.) Buy organic carrots, if you can, because high pesticide residues have been found in nonorganic ones. As an added bonus, organic carrots do not need peeling.

Look for firm, smooth carrots—the smaller they are, the sweeter they are. Carrots should be prepared just before use to preserve their valuable nutrients. They are delicious raw, and can be steamed, stir-fried, roasted, or puréed.

Health Benefits: A single carrot will supply enough vitamin A for an entire day and is reputed to cut the risk of lung cancer by half, even among ex-smokers. According to one American doctor, eating an extra carrot a day could prevent 20,000 lung cancer deaths each year in the United States. This may be due to the high level of the antioxidant beta carotene that carrots contain. Beta carotene may also reduce the risk of prostate cancer in men.

Brightly Colored Vegetables

Ensure there is color in your diet. Beta carotene is just one of the carotenoids found in green, yellow, orange, and red vegetables (as well as fruit). Most carotenoids are antioxidants, which slow down or prevent cell damage from free radical oxidation in the body. Vitamins C and E are other carotenoids, along with bioflavonoids. These help to enhance the immune system, which protects us against viral and bacterial infections and boosts the body's ability to fight cancer and heart disease.

Beet

BEET

Deep, ruby-red in color, beet adds a vibrant hue and flavor to all sorts of dishes. It is often pickled in vinegar, but is much better roasted, as this emphasizes its sweet earthy flavor. Raw beet can be grated into salads or used to make relishes. It can also be added to risottos or made into delicious soups. If cooking beet whole, wash carefully, taking care not to damage the skin or the nutrients and color will leach out. Trim the stalks to about 1 inch above the root. Small beets are sweeter and more tender than larger ones.

Health Benefits: Beet has long been considered medicinally beneficial and is recommended as a general tonic. It can be used to help disorders of the blood, including anemia, it is an effective detoxifier, and, because of its high fiber content, is recommended to relieve constipation. Beet contains calcium, iron, and vitamins A and C—all at their highest levels when it is eaten raw.

CELERY ROOT

This knobby root is closely related to celery, which explains its flavor—a cross between aniseed, celery, and parsley. Similar in size to a small rutabaga, it has ivory flesh and is one of the few root vegetables that must be peeled before use. When grated and eaten raw in salads, celery root has a crunchy texture. It can also be steamed, baked in gratins, or combined with potatoes and mashed with butter or margarine and grainy mustard. It can also be used in soups and broths.

Health Benefits: Like celery, celery root is a diuretic. It also contains vitamin C, calcium, iron, potassium, and fiber.

Rutabaga contains antioxidants and other compounds that may help to prevent cancer

Parsnips

Celery root

RUTABAGA

The globe-shaped rutabaga has pale orange flesh with a delicate sweet flavor. Trim off the thick peel, then treat in the same way as other root vegetables: grate raw into salads; dice and cook in casseroles and soups; or steam, then mash and serve as an accompaniment.

Health Benefits: Rutabagas are part of the cruciferous vegetable family, and contain compounds that are believed to have antioxidant and cancer-fighting properties. They also contain vitamins A and C.

PARSNIP

This vegetable has a sweet, creamy flavor and is delicious roasted, puréed, or steamed. Parsnips are best purchased after the first frost of the year, as the cold converts their starches into sugar, enhancing their sweetness. Scrub before use and peel only if tough. Avoid large roots, which can be woody.

Health Benefits: Parsnips are effective detoxifiers and are believed to fight some cancers. They contain vitamins C and E, iron, folic acid, and potassium.

TURNIPS

This humble root vegetable has many health-giving qualities, and small turnips with their green tops intact are especially nutritious. Their crisp, ivory flesh, which is enclosed in white, green, and pink-tinged skin, has a pleasant, slightly peppery flavor, the intensity of which depends on their size and the time of harvesting. Small turnips can be eaten raw. Alternatively, steam, bake, or use in casseroles and soups.

Health Benefits: This cruciferous vegetable is said to halt the onset of certain cancers, particularly rectal cancer. It is also a digestive and maintains bowel regularity. The green tops are rich in beta carotene and vitamin C.

POTATOES

There are thousands of potato varieties, and many lend themselves to particular cooking methods. Small potatoes, such as Pink Fir Apple and Charlotte, and new potatoes, such as Jersey Royals, are best steamed. They have a waxy texture, which retains its shape after cooking, making them ideal for salads. Main-crop potatoes, such as Red Pontiac and Maris Piper, are more suited to roasting, baking, or mashing, and can be used for

Baby turnips

french fries. Discard any potatoes with green patches as these indicate the presence of toxic alkaloids called solanines.

Vitamins and minerals are stored in, or just below, the skin, so it is best to use

potatoes unpeeled. New potatoes and special salad potatoes need only be scrubbed. Potatoes are not in themselves fattening—it is added ingredients, such as cheese, and the cooking method that can add on the calories. Steam rather than boil, and bake instead of frying to retain valuable nutrients and to keep fat levels down.

Health Benefits: Potatoes are high in complex carbohydrates and include both protein and fiber. They provide plenty of sustained energy, plus vitamins B and C, iron, and potassium.

JERUSALEM ARTICHOKES

This small knobby tuber has a sweet, nutty flavor. Peeling can be awkward, although scrubbing and trimming is usually sufficient. Store in the fridge for up to one week. Use in the same way as potatoes—they make good creamy soups.

Health Benefits: Jerusalem artichokes contain vitamin C and fiber.

COOK'S TIP

To prevent root vegetables and tubers discoloring after preparation, immerse them in a bowl of acidulated water—water containing 1 tablespoon lemon juice. Don't soak them for long because water-soluble vitamins will leach out into the water.

Potatoes

RADISHES

There are several types of this peppery-flavored vegetable, which is a member of the cruciferous family. The round ruby-red variety is most familiar; the longer, white-tipped type has a milder taste. Daikon or mooli radishes are white and very long; they can weigh up to several pounds. Radishes can be used to add both flavor and a crunchy texture to salads and stir-fries. A renowned diuretic, radishes also contain vitamin C.

Jerusalem artichokes

Radishes

Daikon

HORSERADISH

This pungent root is never eaten as a vegetable. It is usually grated and mixed with cream or oil and vinegar, and served as a culinary accompaniment. It is effective in clearing blocked sinuses.

Buying and Storing: Seek out bright, firm, unwrinkled root vegetables and tubers, which do not have soft patches. When possible, choose organically grown produce, and buy in small quantities to ensure freshness. Store root vegetables in a cool, dark place.

Horseradish

Top Tuber

There are two types of the nutritious sweet potato; one has cream flesh, the other orange. The orange-fleshed variety has a higher nutritional content because it is richer in the antioxidant beta carotene, but both types contain potassium, fiber, and vitamin C, as well as providing plenty of sustained energy. Sweet potatoes are thought to cleanse and detoxify the body and can boost poor circulation. When cooked, the cream-fleshed variety has a drier texture. Both are suited to mashing, baking, and roasting.

Basic Vegetable Stock

Stock is easy to make at home and is a healthier option than store-bought stock. It can be stored in the fridge for up to four days. Alternatively, it can be prepared in large quantities and frozen.

INGREDIENTS

1 tablespoon olive oil
1 potato, chopped (½ cup)
1 carrot, chopped (2 tablespoons)
1 onion, chopped (⅔ cup)
1 celery stalk, chopped (1 cup)
2 garlic cloves, peeled
1 sprig of thyme
1 bay leaf
a few stalks of parsley
2½ cups water
salt and freshly ground black pepper

1 Heat the oil in a large saucepan. Add the vegetables and cook, covered, for 10 minutes, or until softened, stirring occasionally. Stir in the garlic and herbs.

2 Pour the water into the pan, bring to a boil, and simmer, partially covered, for 40 minutes. Strain, season with salt and pepper, and use as required.

Brassicas and Green Leafy Vegetables

This large group of vegetables boasts an extraordinary number of health-giving properties. Brassicas range from the crinkly-leafed Savoy cabbage to the small, walnut-sized Brussels sprout. Green, leafy vegetables include spinach, collard greens, and Swiss chard.

Broccoli

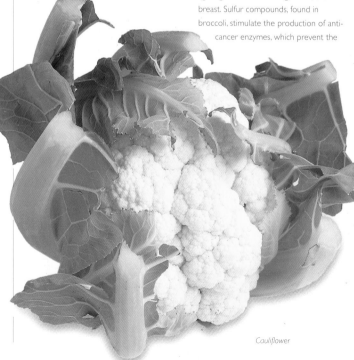

BROCCOLI

This nutritious vegetable should be a regular part of everyone's diet. Two types are commonly available: purple-sprouting, which has fine, leafy stems and a delicate head, and calabrese, the more substantial variety with a tightly budded top and thick stalk. Choose broccoli that has bright, compact flowerets. Yellowing flowerets, a limp woody stalk, and a pungent smell are an indication of overmaturity. Trim stalks before cooking, although young stems can be eaten, too. Serve raw in salads or with a dip. If you cook broccoli, steam or stir-fry it to preserve the nutrients and keep the cooking time brief to retain the vivid green color and crisp texture.

Health Benefits: Broccoli is a member of the cruciferous family, which studies have shown to be particularly effective in fighting cancer of the lung, colon, and breast. Sulfur compounds, found in broccoli, stimulate the production of anti-cancer enzymes, which prevent the growth of tumors and inhibit the spread of existing tumors. Raw broccoli contains almost as much calcium as milk, and also provides plenty of B vitamins, vitamin C, iron, folate, zinc, and potassium.

CAULIFLOWER

The cream-colored compact flowerets should be encased in large, bright green leaves. To get the most nutrients from a cauliflower, eat it raw, or bake, or steam lightly. Cauliflower has a mild flavor and is delicious tossed in a vinaigrette dressing or combined with tomatoes and spices. Overcooked cauliflower is unpleasant and has a sulfurous taste.

Health Benefits: This creamy-white cruciferous vegetable has many cancer-fighting qualities, particularly against cancer of the lung and colon. Cauliflower also contains vitamin C, folate, and potassium and is used in natural medicine as a blood purifier and laxative.

Preparing Broccoli

Trim the stalks from broccoli and divide it into flowerets before using. The stems of young broccoli can be sliced and eaten, too.

Cauliflower

The Crucial Role of Phytochemicals

Cruciferous vegetables, such as broccoli, cabbages, kohlrabi, radishes, cauliflowers, Brussels sprouts, watercress, turnips, kale, bok choy, mustard greens, collard greens, chard, and rutabaga, are all packed with phytochemicals, which numerous studies have shown can fight off various forms of cancer. These are a group of compounds found in varying amounts in all fruit and vegetables, but particularly in cruciferous vegetables.

Phytochemicals are believed to provide an anticarcinogenic cocktail, which plays a crucial role in fighting disease by stimulating the body's enzyme defences against cancer-inducing substances. Eating cruciferous vegetables on a regular basis—

Kohlrabi (below left); Chinese cabbages and cavalo nero (below); and cauliflower, Savoy cabbage, Brussels sprouts, spinach leaves, broccoli, and kale (right) are packed with phytochemicals

at least three or four times a week—may halve the risk of lung, colon, breast, ovary, uterus, or prostate cancer.

According to a senior British researcher, phytochemicals may be found to be as important as antioxidants in fighting disease. Phytochemicals include compounds such as carotenoids, selenium, fiber, isothiocyanates, indoles, phenols, tocopherols, bioflavonoids, and protease inhibitors.

CABBAGE

Frequently overcooked, cabbage is best eaten raw, or cooked until only just tender. There are several different varieties: Savoy cabbage has substantial, crinkly leaves with a strong flavor and is perfect for stuffing; firm white and red cabbages can be shredded and used raw in salads (as can Chinese cabbage); while bok choy is best cooked in stir-fries or with noodles.

Health Benefits: Studies show that eating cabbage more than once a week can reduce the likelihood of colon cancer in men by about 65 percent. Raw or juiced cabbage is particularly potent and has antiviral and antibacterial qualities as well. Cabbage is thought to speed up the metabolism of estrogen in women and this may provide protection against cancer of the breast and uterus. It is a valuable source of vitamins C and E, beta carotene, folate, potassium, thiamine, and fiber.

Cabbage

Mixed Cabbage Stir-fry

Stir-frying is a quick method of cooking that retains much of the vitamins and minerals that are lost during boiling. When cabbage is cooked in this way, it remains crisp and keeps its vivid color.

INGREDIENTS

1 tablespoon peanut or
    sunflower oil
1 large garlic clove, chopped
1-inch piece fresh ginger root, chopped
5 cups mixed cabbage leaves, such as
    Savoy, white, cavalo nero, or
    bok choy, finely shredded
2 teaspoons soy sauce
1 teaspoon clear honey
1 teaspoon toasted sesame oil (optional)
1 tablespoon sesame seeds, toasted

1 Heat the oil in a wok or large, deep skillet, then sauté the garlic and ginger for about 30 seconds. Add the cabbage and stir-fry for 3–5 minutes, until tender, tossing frequently.

2 Stir in the soy sauce, honey, and sesame oil and cook for 1 minute. Sprinkle with sesame seeds and serve.

Health Benefits: Brussels sprouts contain significant amounts of vitamin C, folate, iron, potassium, and some B vitamins. Because they are a cruciferous vegetable, sprouts can help prevent certain cancers.

Buying and Storing: Seek out bright, firm brassicas with no signs of discoloration or wilting. Avoid cauliflowers that have black spots or yellowing leaves. Ensure cabbages have a heavy heart. Chinese cabbages should be compact and heavy for their size with bright, undamaged leaves. Choose small Brussels sprouts with tightly packed leaves. Store cabbages and Brussels sprouts in a cool, dark place for up to a week. Broccoli and cauliflower should be stored in the fridge for only 2–3 days. Chinese cabbage and bok choy don't keep well. Store in the salad drawer of the fridge and use within 1–2 days.

Preparing Brussels Sprouts

1 Peel away any outer damaged leaves from the Brussels sprouts.

2 Before cooking, cut a cross in the base of each sprout, so that they cook quickly and evenly.

BRUSSELS SPROUTS

These are basically miniature cabbages that grow on a long tough stalk. They have a strong nutty flavor. The best are small with tightly packed leaves—avoid any that are very large or turning yellow or brown. Sprouts are sweeter when picked after the first frost. They are best cooked very lightly, so either steam or, better still, stir-fry to keep their green color and crisp texture, as well as to retain the vitamins and minerals.

Brussels sprouts

GREEN LEAFY VEGETABLES

For years we have been told to eat up our greens and now we are beginning to learn why. Research into their health benefits has indicated that eating dark green leafy vegetables, such as spinach, collard greens, chard, and kale, on a regular basis may protect us against certain forms of cancer.

Kale

Swiss chard

A member of the beet family, Swiss chard has large, dark leaves and thick, white, orange or red edible ribs. It can be used in the same way as spinach, or the stems may be cooked on their own. Swiss chard is rich in vitamins and minerals, although, like spinach, it contains oxalic acid.

Spinach

This dark, green leaf is a superb source of cancer-fighting antioxidants. It contains about four times more beta carotene than broccoli. It is also rich in fiber, which can help to lower harmful levels of LDL cholesterol in the body, reducing the risk of heart disease and stroke. Spinach does contain iron, but not in such rich supply as was once thought. Furthermore, spinach contains oxalic acid, which inhibits the absorption of iron and calcium in the body. However, eating spinach with a vitamin-C-rich food will increase absorption. Spinach also contains vitamins C and B_6, calcium, potassium, folate, thiamine, and zinc. Nutritionally, it is most beneficial when eaten raw in a salad, but it is also good lightly steamed, then chopped and added to omelets.

Spinach

Spinach beet

Similar to Swiss chard, this form of the beet plant is grown only for its leaves, which have a sweet, mild flavor. Use in the same way as spinach.

Collard greens

These leafy, dark green young cabbages are full of flavor. Rich in vitamin C and beta carotene, collard greens contain indoles, one of the phytochemicals that are thought to protect the body against breast and ovarian cancer.

Buying and Storing: Green, leafy vegetables do not keep well—up to 2 or 3 days at most. Eat soon after purchase to enjoy them at their best. Look for brightly colored, undamaged leaves that are not showing any signs of yellowing or wilting. Wash the leaves thoroughly in cold water before use and eat them raw, or cook lightly, either by steaming or stir-frying to preserve their valuable nutrients.

Spinach beet

Mixed Swiss chard

Collard greens

Pumpkins and Squashes

Widely popular in the United States, Africa, Australia, and the Caribbean, pumpkins and squashes come in a tremendous range of shapes, colors, and sizes. Squashes are broadly divided into summer and winter types: cucumbers and zucchini fall into the summer category, while pumpkins, butternut, and acorn squashes are winter varieties.

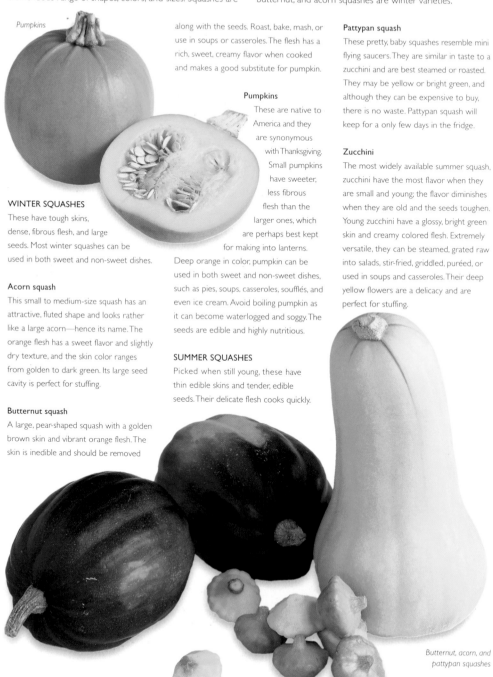

Pumpkins

along with the seeds. Roast, bake, mash, or use in soups or casseroles. The flesh has a rich, sweet, creamy flavor when cooked and makes a good substitute for pumpkin.

Pumpkins

These are native to America and they are synonymous with Thanksgiving. Small pumpkins have sweeter, less fibrous flesh than the larger ones, which are perhaps best kept for making into lanterns. Deep orange in color, pumpkin can be used in both sweet and non-sweet dishes, such as pies, soups, casseroles, soufflés, and even ice cream. Avoid boiling pumpkin as it can become waterlogged and soggy. The seeds are edible and highly nutritious.

SUMMER SQUASHES

Picked when still young, these have thin edible skins and tender, edible seeds. Their delicate flesh cooks quickly.

Pattypan squash

These pretty, baby squashes resemble mini flying saucers. They are similar in taste to a zucchini and are best steamed or roasted. They may be yellow or bright green, and although they can be expensive to buy, there is no waste. Pattypan squash will keep for a only few days in the fridge.

Zucchini

The most widely available summer squash, zucchini have the most flavor when they are small and young; the flavor diminishes when they are old and the seeds toughen. Young zucchini have a glossy, bright green skin and creamy colored flesh. Extremely versatile, they can be steamed, grated raw into salads, stir-fried, griddled, puréed, or used in soups and casseroles. Their deep yellow flowers are a delicacy and are perfect for stuffing.

WINTER SQUASHES

These have tough skins, dense, fibrous flesh, and large seeds. Most winter squashes can be used in both sweet and non-sweet dishes.

Acorn squash

This small to medium-size squash has an attractive, fluted shape and looks rather like a large acorn—hence its name. The orange flesh has a sweet flavor and slightly dry texture, and the skin color ranges from golden to dark green. Its large seed cavity is perfect for stuffing.

Butternut squash

A large, pear-shaped squash with a golden brown skin and vibrant orange flesh. The skin is inedible and should be removed

Butternut, acorn, and pattypan squashes

Zucchini

to use raw in salads or thinly sliced as a sandwich filling. However, they can also be pickled and cooked in other ways, such as steaming, baking, or stir-frying.

Buying and Storing: Look for firm, bright, unblemished vegetables that are heavy for their size. Winter squash can be kept for several weeks if stored whole in a cool, dry place. Once cut, they should be kept in the fridge and eaten as soon as possible. Summer squash don't keep as well and should be stored in the fridge for only a few days.

Squash

The grown-up equivalent of zucchini, this squash has a pleasant, mild flavor and is best baked either plain or with a stuffing. Spices, chile peppers, and tomatoes are particularly good flavorings.

Cucumbers

Probably cultivated as long ago as 10,000 BC, cucumbers were popular vegetables with the Greeks and the Romans. The long, thin, smooth-skinned variety is most familiar. Their refreshing, mild flavor makes cucumbers perfect

Squash

Peeling Pumpkin

1 Cut the pumpkin in half using a large sharp knife and scoop out the seeds and fibrous parts with a spoon.

2 Cut the pumpkin into large chunks, then cut the skin using a sharp knife.

Roasting Squash

1 Preheat the oven to 400°F. Cut the squash in half, scoop out the seeds and place the squash cut side down on an oiled cookie sheet.

2 Bake for 30 minutes, or until the flesh is soft. Serve in the skin, or remove the flesh and mash with butter.

Health Benefits:
Summer squash are effective diuretics and their potassium content means they are beneficial for those with high blood pressure. Pumpkins are also a diuretic, as well as a laxative, and like other winter squashes, contain high amounts of vitamin E, beta carotene, and potassium. Beta carotene and vitamin E are antioxidants and are believed to reduce the risk of certain cancers. Summer squashes contain less beta carotene. Because of their high water content, all squash are low in calories.

Cucumber

Vegetables

Shoot Vegetables

This highly prized collection of vegetables, each honored with a distinctive flavor and appearance, ranges from the aristocratic asparagus to the flowerbud-like globe artichoke.

FENNEL

Florence fennel is closely related to the herb and spice of the same name. The short, fat bulbs have a similar texture to celery and are topped with edible feathery fronds. Fennel has a mild aniseed flavor, which is most potent when eaten raw. Cooking tempers the flavor, giving it a delicious sweetness. When using fennel raw, slice it thinly or chop roughly and add to salads. Alternatively, slice or cut into wedges and steam, or brush with olive oil and roast, or cook on a griddle. Fennel is at its best when it is fresh and should be eaten as soon as possible. It can, however, be stored in the fridge for a few days.

Asparagus

Health Benefits:

Fennel is a diuretic and also has a calming and toning effect on the stomach. It is low in calories and contains beta carotene and folate, which is known to reduce the risk of spina bifida in the unborn child. Fennel seeds are good for the digestion.

ASPARAGUS

Highly valued since Roman times, asparagus has been cultivated commercially since the 17th century. There are two main types: white asparagus is picked just before it sprouts above the surface of the soil; while green-tipped asparagus is cut above the ground and develops its color when it comes into contact with sunlight. It takes three years to grow a crop from seed, which may account for its expense. Before use, scrape the lower half of the stalk with a vegetable peeler, then trim off the woody end.

Briefly poach whole spears in a skillet containing a little boiling salted water, or tie the spears in a bundle and boil upright in an asparagus boiler or tall pan. Asparagus is delicious served with melted butter, or dipped into mayonnaise or vinaigrette. It can also be roasted in a little olive oil and served with a sprinkling of sea salt to bring out the flavor.

Health Benefits: Asparagus was used as a medicine long before it was eaten as a food. It is a rich source of vitamin C and also has diuretic and laxative properties. It contains the antioxidant glutathione, which has been found to prevent the formation of cataracts in the eyes.

White and red Belgian endive

Preparing Fennel

Cut the fennel bulb in half lengthwise, then either cut into quarters or slice thinly.

Fennel

BELGIAN ENDIVE

This shoot has long, tightly packed leaves. There are two kinds, white and red. Red Belgian endive has a more pronounced flavor, while the white variety has crisper leaves. The crisp texture and slightly bitter flavor means that it is particularly good in salads. It can also be steamed or braised, although in cooking, sadly, the red-leaf

Health Benefits: Globe artichokes are a good source of vitamins A and C, fiber, iron, calcium, and potassium. In natural medicine, they are used to treat high blood pressure.

Buying and Storing: When buying shoot vegetables, always choose the freshest-looking specimens. Asparagus spears should have firm stalks. Belgian endive should be neither withered nor brown at the edges—the best white variety is sold wrapped in blue paper to keep out the sunlight and to prevent it from turning green and bitter. Fennel bulbs should be crisp and white with fresh fronds. Globe artichokes should have tightly closed, stiff leaves and the stalk attached.

Store all these vegetables in the salad drawer of the fridge. Asparagus, Belgian endive, and fennel should be eaten within 2–3 days; globe artichokes will keep for up to a week; and celery will keep for about 2 weeks if very fresh when purchased.

Left: Globe artichokes, celery, and Belgian endive

variety fades to brown. Before use, remove the outer leaves and wash thoroughly, then trim the base. In natural medicine, Belgian endive is sometimes used to treat gout and rheumatism. It is also a digestive and liver stimulant, and good for a spring tonic.

CELERY

Like asparagus, celery was once grown primarily for medicinal reasons. Serve raw, steam, or braise. Celery leaves have a tangy taste and are also useful for adding flavor to stocks. Low in calories, but rich in vitamin C and potassium, celery is a recognized diuretic and sedative.

GLOBE ARTICHOKES

Once cooked, the purple-tinged leaves of globe artichokes have an exquisite flavor. They are eaten with the fingers by dipping each leaf into garlic butter or vinaigrette dressing, then drawing each leaf through the teeth and eating the fleshy part. The heart is then dipped in the butter or dressing and eaten with a knife and fork.

Preparing Globe Artichokes

1 Hold the top of the artichoke firmly and using a sharp knife, remove the stalk, and trim the base so that the artichoke sits flat.

3 Cook the artichokes in a pan of boiling, lightly salted water for 35–45 minutes, until a leaf can be pulled out easily. Drain upside down.

2 Using a sharp knife or scissors, trim off and discard the tops of the leaves and cut off the pointed top.

4 Pull out the central leaves, then scoop out the hairy choke with a teaspoon, and discard.

Vegetable Fruits

By cultivation and use, tomatoes, eggplant, and bell peppers are all vegetables, but botanically they are classified as fruit. Part of the nightshade family, they have only relatively recently become appreciated for their health-giving qualities.

Tomatoes

TOMATOES

There are dozens of varieties to choose from, which vary in color, shape, and size. The egg-shaped plum tomato is perfect for cooking as it has a rich flavor and a high proportion of flesh to seeds—but it must be used when fully ripe. Too often, store-bought tomatoes are bland and tasteless because they have been picked too young. Vine-ripened and cherry tomatoes are sweet and juicy and are good in salads or uncooked sauces. Large beefsteak tomatoes have a good flavor and are also excellent for salads. Sun-dried tomatoes add a rich intensity to sauces, soups, and stews. Genetically engineered tomatoes are now sold in some countries, but at present they are only sold canned as a concentrated paste. Check the label before buying.

EGGPLANT

The dark-purple, glossy-skinned eggplant is the most familiar variety, although it was the small, ivory-white egg-shaped variety that originally inspired the name eggplant. There is also the bright-green pea eggplant that is used in Asian cooking, and a pale-purple Chinese eggplant. Known in the Middle East as "poor man's caviar," eggplants give substance and flavor to spicy casseroles and tomato-based bakes, and are delicious roasted, griddled, and

Buying and Storing:
Look for deep-red fruit with a firm, yielding flesh. Tomatoes that are grown and sold locally will have the best flavor. To improve the flavor of a slightly hard tomato, leave it to ripen fully at room temperature. Avoid refrigeration because this stops the ripening process and adversely affects the taste and texture of the tomato.

Health Benefits: Vine-ripened tomatoes are higher in vitamin C than those picked when they are still green. They are also a good source of vitamin E, beta carotene, magnesium, calcium, and phosphorus. Tomatoes contain the bioflavonoid lycopene, which is believed to prevent some forms of cancer by reducing the harmful effects of free radicals.

Eggplant

Peeling and Seeding Tomatoes

Tomato seeds can give sauces a bitter flavor. Removing them and the tomato skins will also give a smoother end result.

2 Lift out the tomatoes with a slotted spoon, rinse in cold water to cool slightly, and peel away the skin.

1 Immerse the tomatoes in boiling water and leave for about 30 seconds—the base of each tomato can be slashed to make peeling easier.

3 Cut the tomatoes in half, then scoop out the seeds, and remove the hard core. Dice or roughly chop the flesh according to the recipe.

puréed into garlic-laden dips. It is not essential to salt eggplant to remove any bitterness; however, this method prevents the absorption of excessive amounts of oil during frying.

Buying and Storing: When buying, look for small to medium-size eggplant, which have sweet, tender flesh. Large specimens with a shriveled skin are overmature and are likely to be bitter and tough. Store in the fridge for up to two weeks.

Health Benefits: An excellent source of vitamin C, eggplant also contain moderate amounts of iron and potassium, calcium, and B vitamins. They also contain bioflavonoids, which help prevent strokes and reduce the risk of certain cancers.

Bird's eye chile peppers

Serrano chile peppers

Habanero chile peppers

CHILE PEPPERS

Native to America, this member of the capsicum family now forms an important part of many cuisines, including Indian, Thai, Mexican, South American, and African. There are more than 200 different types of chile pepper, ranging from the long, narrow Anaheim to the lantern-shaped and incredibly hot Habanero. Red chile peppers are not necessarily hotter than green ones—but they will probably have ripened for longer in the sun. The heat in chiles comes from capsaicin, a compound found in the seeds, white membranes, and, to a lesser extent, in the flesh. Chile peppers range in potency from the mild and flavorful to the blisteringly hot. Dried chiles tend to be hotter than fresh. Smaller chiles, such as Bird's eye chiles, contain more seeds and membrane, which makes them more potent than larger ones. It is

important to wash your hands after using chile peppers as they can irritate the skin and eyes.

Buying and Storing: Choose unwrinkled firm chile peppers and store in the fridge.

Health Benefits: Chile peppers contain more vitamin C than an orange and are a good source of beta carotene, folate, potassium, and vitamin E. They stimulate the release of endorphins, the body's "feel-good" chemicals and are a powerful decongestant, helping to open sinuses and air passages. Chiles stimulate the body and improve circulation, but if eaten to excess, can irritate the stomach.

Chile Boost

For an instant uplift, sprinkle some dried crushed chile on your food. The chile will stimulate the release of endorphins, which are the body's "feel-good" chemicals.

Handle chile peppers with care, as they can irritate the skin and eyes. Wear gloves when preparing chiles.

Red and green chile peppers

Jalapeño chile peppers

Avocados

Although avocados have a high fat content, the fat is monounsaturated, and is thought to lower blood cholesterol levels in the body. Avocados also contain valuable amounts of vitamins C and E, and iron, potassium, and manganese. They are said to improve the condition of the skin and hair.

Once cut, avocados should be brushed with lemon or lime juice to prevent discoloration. They are usually eaten raw. Avocado halves can be dressed with a vinaigrette, or filled with sour cream sprinkled with cayenne pepper, or hummus. Slices or chunks of avocado are delicious in salads. In Mexico, where they grow in abundance, there are countless dishes based on avocados. Guacamole is the best known, but they are also used in soups and stews.

BELL PEPPERS

Like chiles, bell peppers are also members of the capsicum family. They range in color from green through to orange, yellow, red, and even purple. Green bell peppers are fully developed, but not completely ripe, which can make them difficult to digest. They have refreshing, juicy flesh with a crisp texture. Other colors of bell peppers are more mature, have sweeter flesh, and are more digestible than less ripe green ones.

Peeling Bell Peppers

1 Roast the bell peppers under a hot broiler for 12–15 minutes, turning regularly until the skin chars and blisters.

2 Alternatively, place on a cookie sheet and roast in an oven preheated to 400°F for 20–30 minutes, until blackened and blistered.

Roasting or charbroiling bell peppers will enhance their sweetness. They can also be stuffed, sliced into salads, or steamed.

Buying and Storing: Choose bell peppers that are firm and glossy with unblemished skin, and store in the fridge for up to a week.

Health Benefits: Bell peppers contain significant amounts of vitamin C, as well as beta carotene, some B complex vitamins, calcium, phosphorus, and iron.

3 Put the bell peppers in a plastic bag and let cool—the steam will encourage the skin to peel away easily.

4 Peel away the skin, then slice in half. Remove the core and scrape out any remaining seeds. Slice or chop according to the recipe.

Bell peppers

Pods and Seeds

While most of these vegetables are delicious eaten fresh, many of them—peas, corn, and fava and green beans, for example—can also be bought frozen. High in nutritional value, these popular vegetables can be enjoyed all year. Other types of pea include snow peas and sugar snap peas, which can be eaten whole—pod and all.

Above, clockwise from top left: String beans, fine green beans, snow peas, fava beans, peas, and (center) baby corn cobs

PEAS

Peas are one of the few vegetables that taste just as good when frozen. Because freezing takes place soon after picking, frozen peas often have a higher nutritional value than fresh. Another advantage is that frozen peas are readily available all year round. Peas in the pod have a restricted availability and their taste diminishes if not absolutely fresh, because their sugars rapidly turn to starch. However, when they are at the peak of freshness, peas are delicious and have a delicate, sweet flavor. Pop them from the pod and serve raw in salads or steam lightly. Delicious cooked with fresh mint, peas also make satisfying purées and soups, and can be added to risottos and other rice dishes.

FAVA BEANS

When young and fresh these beans are a delight to eat. Tiny pods can be eaten whole; simply trim them, and then slice. Usually, however, you will need to shell the beans, as their skins can become tough. Elderly beans are often better skinned after they are cooked. Fava beans can be eaten raw or lightly cooked.

GREEN BEANS

Green, string, and thin beans are eaten pod and all. They should be bright green and crisp-textured. Simply trim and lightly cook or steam them. Serve green beans hot, or let cool slightly and serve them as a warm salad with a squeeze of fresh lemon juice or with a vinaigrette dressing.

Buying and Storing: Look for bright green, smooth, plump pods and keep in the fridge for no more than a day or two.

Health Benefits: Peas and beans are good sources of protein and fiber. They are rich in vitamin C, iron, thiamine, folate, phosphorous, and potassium.

CORN

Corn cobs are best eaten soon after picking, before their natural sugars start to convert into starch when the flavor fades and the kernels toughen. Remove the green outer leaves and cook whole or slice off the kernels with a sharp knife. Baby corn cobs can be eaten raw, and are good in stir-fries.

Buying and Storing: Look for very fresh, plump kernels that show no signs of discoloration, wrinkling, or drying and eat soon after purchase. If you do not intend to eat them immediately, store in the coolest part of the fridge.

Health Benefits: Corn is a good carbohydrate food and is rich in vitamins A, B, and C, and fiber. It contains useful amounts of iron, magnesium, phosphorus, and potassium. Baby corn is high in folate, which is essential for maintaining the immune system.

Corn

The Onion Family

Onions and garlic are highly prized as two of the oldest remedies known to man. Both contain allicin, which has been found to stimulate the body's antioxidant mechanisms, raising levels of beneficial HDL cholesterol and combating the formation of clogged arteries. Additionally, these vegetables are indispensable in cooking. The wide variety of onions can be enjoyed raw or cooked and, with garlic, add flavor to a huge range of non-sweet dishes.

ONIONS

Every cuisine in the world includes onions in one form or another. They are an essential flavoring, offering a range of taste sensations, from the sweet and juicy red onion and powerfully pungent white onion to the light and fresh scallion. Pearl onions and shallots are the babies of the family. Tiny pearl onions are generally pickled, while shallots are good roasted with their skins on, when they develop a caramel sweetness. Yellow onions are most common and are highly versatile.

Buying and Storing: When buying, choose onions that have dry, papery skins and are heavy for their size. They will keep for 1–2 months stored in a cool, dark place.

Health Benefits: Numerous studies highlight the healing powers of the onion. It is a rich source of quercetin, a potent antioxidant that has been linked to preventing stomach cancer. Eating half a raw onion a day is said to thin the blood, lower the LDL cholesterol, and raise beneficial HDL cholesterol by about 30 percent. This means that cholesterol is transported away from the arteries, reducing the risk of heart disease and stroke. Whether raw or cooked, onions are antibacterial and antiviral, helping to fight off colds, relieve bronchial congestion, asthma, and hay fever. They are also good for people with arthritis, rheumatism, and gout.

GARLIC

For centuries, this wonder food has been the focus of much attention, and is praised for its medicinal powers, which range from curing toothache to warding off evil demons. The flavor of garlic is milder when whole or sliced; crushing or chopping releases the oils, making the flavor stronger. Slow-cooking also tames the pungency of garlic, although it still affects the breath.

Onion and Garlic Cures

Onions have been used in all kinds of traditional remedies.
• In the past, babies were often given a teaspoonful of onion infusion for colic: a slice of onion would be infused in hot water for a few minutes, and the water let cool.
• Raw garlic can relieve symptoms of food poisoning. It has been shown to kill bacteria, even those that are resistant to antibiotics. Some people say that garlic keeps old age at bay.

Buying and Storing: Most garlic is semi-dried to prolong its shelf life, yet the cloves should still be moist and juicy. Young garlic, which is available in early summer, has a long green stem and soft white bulb. It has a fresher flavor than semi-dried garlic, but can be used in the same ways. Pungency varies, but the general rule when buying garlic is: the smaller the bulb, the more potent the flavor. If stored in a cool, dry place and not in

Above: Scallions, red onions, shallots, and white onions

Leeks

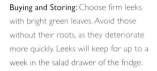

the fridge,
garlic will keep for up to about eight
weeks. If the air is damp, garlic will sprout,
and if it is too warm, the cloves will
eventually turn to gray powder.

Health Benefits: Garlic tops the American
National Cancer Institute's list as a
potential cancer-preventive food. Although
the antiviral, antibacterial, and antifungal
qualities of garlic are most potent when
eaten raw, cooking does not inhibit its
anti-cancer, blood-thinning, and
decongestant capabilities. Studies show
that eating 2–3 garlic cloves a day reduces
by half the probability of a subsequent
heart attack in previous heart patients.
Garlic has also been found to lower blood
cholesterol, reduce high blood pressure,
boost the immune system, act as an anti-
inflammatory, lift mood, and have a calming
effect. It should be eaten on a daily basis.

Below: Garlic bulbs and cloves

LEEKS

Like onions and garlic,
leeks have a very long
history. They grow in all sorts
of climates and are known
to have been eaten and
enjoyed by the ancient
Egyptians, Greeks, and
Romans. Leeks are very versatile, having
their own distinct, subtle flavor. They are
less pungent than onions, but are still
therapeutically beneficial. Excellent in
soups and casseroles, leeks can also be
used as a pie filling or in tarts, or simply
steamed and served hot with a light,
creamy sauce, or cooled slightly and
dressed with a vinaigrette. They are also
delicious sliced or shredded and then stir-
fried with a little garlic and ginger.

Commercially grown leeks are usually
about 10 inches long, but you may
occasionally see baby leeks, which are very
tender and are best steamed.

Buying and Storing: Choose firm leeks
with bright green leaves. Avoid those
without their roots, as they deteriorate
more quickly. Leeks will keep for up to a
week in the salad drawer of the fridge.

Health Benefits: Leeks have the same
active constituents as onions, but in
smaller amounts. They also
contain vitamins C and E,
iron, folate, and
potassium.

Cleaning Leeks

Leeks need meticulous cleaning to remove
any grit and earth that may hide between
the layers of leaves. This method will
ensure that the very last tiny piece of grit
will be washed away.

1 Cut off the root, then trim the top of
the green part and discard. Remove any
tough or damaged outer leaves.

2 Slash the top green part of the leek
into quarters and rinse the leek well
under cold running water, separating the
layers to remove any hidden dirt. Slice or
leave whole, depending on the recipe.

Mushrooms

Thanks to their rich earthiness, mushrooms add substance and flavor to all sorts of dishes. There are more than 2,000 edible varieties, but only a tiny proportion are readily available. These fall into three camps: common cultivated mushrooms, like the button; wild varieties that are now cultivated, such as the shiitake; and the truly wild types that have escaped cultivation, such as the morel.

Cultivated mushrooms come in a wide variety of sizes

BUTTON, CAP, AND FLAT MUSHROOMS

The most common cultivated variety of mushrooms, these are actually one type in various stages of maturity. The button mushroom is the youngest and has, as its name suggests, a tight, white, button-like cap. It has a mild flavor and can be eaten raw in salads. Cap mushrooms are slightly more mature and larger in size, while the flat mushroom is the largest and has dark, open gills. Flat mushrooms have the most prominent flavor and are good broiled or baked on their own, or stuffed.

Chanterelles

Below: Field blewitts

Below: Crimini (left) and portabello mushrooms

CRIMINI MUSHROOMS

The brown-capped crimini mushroom looks similar to the cultivated button, but has a more assertive, nutty flavor.

PORTABELLO MUSHROOMS

Similar in appearance to the cultivated flat mushroom, the portabello is simply a large crimini mushroom. It has a rich flavor and a meaty texture and is good broiled.

FIELD MUSHROOMS

This wild mushroom has an intense, rich flavor. It is ideal for broiling and stuffing.

CHANTERELLES

This egg-yolk-colored mushroom has a pretty, funnel shape and a fragrant but delicate flavor. Also known as the girolle, it is sold fresh in season and dried all year round. If buying fresh, eat as soon as possible and wipe rather than wash, as the skin is very porous. Sauté, bake, or add to sauces.

FIELD BLEWITTS

This wild mushroom is now widely cultivated in caves in Britain, Switzerland, and France. It has a thick, lilac-blue stem,

Dried and fresh cèpes

which is topped with a smooth, whitish cap. When cooked, field blewitts have a dense, meaty texture.

CEPES

This wild mushroom, which is also known by its Italian name, porcini, has a tender, meaty texture and woody flavor. Dried cèpes are used for their rich flavor.

MORELS

Slightly sweet-flavored mushrooms with a distinctive, pointed, honeycomb cap and a hollow stalk, morels can be awkward to clean. They are costly to buy fresh because they have a short season, but can be bought dried.

Shiitake Mushrooms

In Asia, these mushrooms are recommended for a long and healthy life, and research has shown that they have antiviral properties that stimulate the immune system. Shiitake mushrooms may help lower blood cholesterol, even curtailing some of the side effects of saturated fat. They have also been found to halt the later stages of certain cancers.

ENOKI MUSHROOMS

These Japanese mushrooms have a pretty, tiny cap on an elegant, long stalk. Sold in clusters, enoki have a slightly lemony flavor. Use in stir-fries or eat raw in salads.

Dried Mushrooms

These are a useful stand-by and have a rich, intense flavor. To reconstitute dried mushrooms, soak them in boiling water for 20–30 minutes, depending on the variety and size of mushroom, until tender. Drain and rinse well to remove any grit and dirt. Dried mushrooms often require longer cooking than fresh ones.

Morels

OYSTER MUSHROOMS

Now cultivated and widely available, oyster mushrooms have an attractive shell-shaped cap and thick stalk. They are usually pale, gray-brown, although yellow and pink varieties are also available.

Buying and Storing: Buy mushrooms that smell and look fresh. Avoid ones with damp, slimy patches and any that are discolored. Store in a paper bag in the fridge for up to 4 days.

Health Benefits: Mushrooms do not contain a wealth of nutrients but they are a useful source of vitamins B_1 and B_2, potassium, iron, and niacin.

Cleaning Mushrooms: Before use, wipe mushrooms with damp paper towels and trim the stem. Wild mushrooms often harbor grit and dirt and may need to be rinsed briefly under cold running water, but dry thoroughly. Never soak mushrooms or they will become soggy. Peeling is not usually necessary.

Oyster mushrooms

Salad Greens

It is only a few years since the most exotic lettuce available was the crisp-textured iceberg. Today, salad greens come in a huge variety of shapes, sizes, colors, and flavors, from bitter-tasting chicory to peppery arugula and red-leaf lollo rosso. Making a mixed leaf salad has never been so easy, or the result so delicious.

Left, clockwise from left: chicory, oak leaf, romaine, butterhead, and iceberg lettuces

LETTUCES

Cultivated for thousands of years, lettuces were probably first eaten as a salad vegetable during Roman times. Nutritionally, lettuce is best eaten raw, but it can be braised, steamed, or made into a soup. Large-leaf varieties can be used to wrap around a filling.

Butterhead lettuce

This soft-leaf lettuce has an unassuming flavor and is good as a sandwich-filler.

Romaine lettuce

Known since Roman times, the romaine lettuce has long, sturdy leaves and a strong flavor. Little gem is a baby version and has firm, densely packed leaves.

Iceberg lettuce

This lettuce has a round, firm head of pale green leaves with a crisp texture. Like the butterhead, it has a mild, slightly bitter flavor and is best used as a garnish. It is reputed to be one of the most highly chemically treated crops, so choose organic iceberg lettuces if you can.

Oak leaf

This attractive lettuce has red-tinged, soft-textured leaves with a slightly bitter flavor. In salads, combine with green lettuces for a contrast of tastes and textures.

Lollo rosso

The pretty, frilly leaves of lollo rosso are green at the base and a deep, fall red around the edge. Its imposing shape means it is best mixed with other leaves if used in a salad, or as a base for roasted vegetables. Lollo biondo is a pale green version.

Chicory

Also known as frisée, chicory has spiky, ragged leaves that are dark green on the outside and fade to an attractive pale yellow-green towards its center. It has a distinctive bitter flavor that is enhanced by a robust dressing.

Radicchio

Mâche

Sorrel

Arugula

Mâche

Also known as corn salad, this tiny lettuce has a cluster of small, rounded, velvety leaves with a delicate flavor. Serve on its own or mix with other salad greens.

SALAD GREENS

A great variety of different salad greens is now readily available.

Radicchio

A member of the chicory family, radicchio has deep red, tightly packed leaves that have a bitter peppery flavor. It is good in salads and can be sautéed or roasted.

Arugula

Classified as a herb, arugula is a popular addition to salads, or it can be served as a starter with thin shavings of Parmesan cheese. It has a strong, peppery flavor, which is more robust when wild. Lightly steamed arugula has a milder flavor than the raw leaves, but it is equally delicious.

Sorrel

The long pointed leaves of sorrel have a refreshing, sharp flavor that is best when mixed with milder tasting leaves. It contains oxalic acid which, when cooked, inhibits the absorption of iron. Sorrel is an effective diuretic.

Watercress

The hot, peppery flavor of watercress complements milder tasting leaves and is classically combined with fresh orange. It does not keep well and is best used within two days of purchase. Watercress is a member of the cruciferous family and shares its cancer-fighting properties.

Buying and Storing: Salad greens are best when they are very fresh and do not keep well. Avoid leaves that are wilted, discolored, or shriveled. Store in the fridge, unwashed, for between 2 days and 1 week, depending on the variety. As salad greens are routinely sprayed with pesticides, they should be washed thoroughly, but gently, to avoid damaging the leaves, and then dried in a dish towel. Better still, choose organically grown produce.

Health Benefits: Although all types of salad greens are about 90 percent water, they contain useful amounts of vitamins and minerals, particularly folate, iron, and the antioxidants, vitamin C and beta carotene. The outer, darker leaves tend to be more nutritious than the paler leaves in the center. More importantly, like other green, leafy vegetables, their antioxidant content has been found to guard against the risk of many cancers. Salad greens are usually eaten raw, when the nutrients are at their strongest. Lettuce is reputed to have a calming, sedative effect.

Watercress

Herbs

Herbs have been highly prized by natural practitioners for centuries because, in spite of their low nutritional value, they possess many reputed healing qualities. In cooking, herbs can make a significant difference to the flavor and aroma of a dish and they have the ability to enliven the simplest of meals. Fresh herbs can easily be grown at home in the garden, or in a pot, or window box.

Chives and bay leaves

BASIL

This delicate aromatic herb is widely used in Italian and Thai cooking. The leaves bruise easily, so are best used whole or torn, rather than cut with a knife. Basil is said to have a calming effect on the stomach, easing constipation, nausea, and cramps, and aiding digestion.

BAY LEAVES

These dark-green, glossy leaves are best left to dry for a few days before use. They have a robust, spicy flavor and are an essential ingredient in bouquet garni. Studies show that bay has a restorative effect on the digestive system.

CHIVES

A member of the onion family, chives have a milder flavor and are best used as a garnish, snipped over egg or potato dishes, or added to salads or tarts. Like onions, chives are an antiseptic and act as a digestive.

CILANTRO

Warm and spicy, cilantro is popular in Indian and Thai curries, stir-fries, and salads. It looks similar to flat leaf parsley, but its taste is completely different. It is often sold with its root intact. The root has a more intense flavor than the leaves and can be used in curry pastes. Cilantro

Using Dried Herbs

Although fresh herbs have the best flavor and appearance, dried herbs can be a convenient and useful alternative, especially in the winter months when some fresh herbs are not available.

• A few herbs, such as basil, dill, mint, and parsley do not dry well, losing most of their flavor.

• Oregano, thyme, marjoram, and bay retain their flavor when dried and are useful substitutes for fresh.

• Dried herbs have a more concentrated flavor than fresh, so much less is required—usually a third to a half as much as fresh.

• When using dried herbs in cooking, always allow sufficient time for them to rehydrate and soften.

• Dried herbs do little for uncooked dishes, but are useful for flavoring marinades, and are good in slow-cooked stews and soups.

• When buying dried herbs, they should look bright, not faded. Because light spoils their flavor and shortens shelf-life, store in sealed, airtight jars in a cool, dark place.

Basil

Cilantro

Dill

marinades and is a good partner for mustard. An attractive herb with delicate, wispy leaves, add to dishes just prior to serving as its mild flavor diminishes with cooking. Dill is a popular herb for settling the stomach and is thought to reduce flatulence. It is also said to be mildly soporific and, in the form of gripe water, is sometimes given to babies to relieve gas and colic.

is an effective digestive, easing indigestion and nausea. It is also said to act as a tonic for the heart.

DILL

The mild, yet distinctive, aniseed flavor of dill goes well with potatoes, zucchini, and cucumber. It makes a good addition to creamy sauces and can be added to a wide variety of egg dishes. It can also be used as a flavoring for dressings and

Pesto

Freshly made pesto, spooned over warm pasta or spread over bread and topped with a round of goat cheese, makes a perfect quick supper. It is usually made with basil, but other herbs, such as arugula, cilantro, or parsley, can be substituted. The pine nuts can also be replaced with walnuts, cashew nuts or pistachios.

INGREDIENTS
1 cup fresh basil leaves
2 garlic cloves, crushed
1/2 cup pine nuts
1/2 cup olive oil, plus extra
    for drizzling
4 tablespoons freshly grated
    Parmesan cheese
salt and freshly ground black pepper

1 Place the basil, garlic, and pine nuts in a food processor or blender and process until finely chopped.

2 Gradually add the olive oil and then the Parmesan, and blend to a coarse purée. Season to taste. Spoon into a lidded jar, then pour in the extra olive oil to cover. Use at once or store in the fridge.

Freezing Herbs

This is an excellent method of preserving fresh delicate herbs, such as basil, chives, dill, tarragon, cilantro, and parsley. The herbs will lose their fresh appearance and texture when frozen, but are still suitable for use in cooking. They will keep for up to 3 months in the freezer.

• Half-fill ice-cube trays with chopped herbs and top up with water. Freeze, then place the cubes in freezer-bags. The frozen cubes can be added to soups, stews, and stocks, and heated until they melt.

• Place whole sprigs or leaves, or chopped herbs in freezer bags, expel any air and tightly seal.

• Freeze herb sprigs or leaves on trays. When the herbs are frozen, transfer them carefully to freezer-bags, expel any air, seal tightly, and return to the freezer.

• Pack chopped fresh herbs in plastic containers and freeze. Scatter straight into soups and stews.

Kaffir lime leaves

KAFFIR LIME LEAVES

These attractive glossy, green leaves are commonly used in Asian cuisines, lending a tantalizing citrus aroma and flavor to a wide variety of dishes. They are available fresh from Asian stores, or dried from large supermarkets. The fruit resembles a knobby lime and its rind, which is rich in vitamin C, is used grated in Thai and Indonesian curries. The leaves can be used as a digestive.

LEMON BALM

This herb makes a refreshing tea and is good in any sweet or non-sweet dish that uses lemon juice. It has antibacterial, antiviral, and antidepressant qualities. The calming and sedative attributes of lemon balm are beneficial for those suffering from stress or nervous exhaustion.

MARJORAM

Closely related to oregano, marjoram has a slightly sweeter flavor. It goes well in Mediterranean-style vegetable dishes, such as ratatouille, or in casseroles, and tomato sauces, but should be added at the last minute, as its flavor diminishes when heated. It also makes a good addition to a marinade. Marjoram improves the circulation and relieves stomach pains.

MINT

The most familiar types are spearmint and peppermint, but there are other distinctly flavored varieties, such as apple, lemon, and pineapple mint, which are worth looking for, and make a refreshing drink when infused in boiling water. Mint is used as a flavoring in a wide variety of dishes, from stuffings to fruit salads. It is a vital ingredient in the Middle Eastern salad, tabbouleh, and is also mixed with unsweetened yogurt to make raita, a soothing accompaniment to hot curries. It is a traditional cure for nausea and indigestion and is also effective in stimulating and cleansing the system.

Lemon balm, marjoram, mint, and oregano

OREGANO

This is a wild variety of marjoram, but has a more robust flavor that goes well with tomato-based dishes. Oregano can relieve digestive problems.

PARSLEY

There are two types of parsley: flat leaf and curly. Both taste relatively similar, but the flat leaf variety is preferable in cooked dishes. Parsley is an excellent source of vitamin C, iron, and calcium. Chewing parsley after eating garlic or onions can neutralize the smell and freshen breath.

Parsley

ROSEMARY

Wonderfully aromatic, rosemary is traditionally used in meat dishes, but it can also add a smoky flavor to hearty bean and vegetable dishes. Rosemary has a reputation for invigorating the circulation, and for relieving headaches and respiratory problems.

Rosemary and sage

SAGE

The leaves of this herb, which may be silver-gray or purple, have a potent aroma and only a small amount is needed. Sage is commonly added to meat dishes but, if used discreetly, it is delicious with beans,

cheese, lentils, and in stuffings. Sage was used medicinally before it found its way into the kitchen and is regarded as a tonic for the stomach, kidneys, and liver.

Thyme

THYME

This robustly flavored aromatic herb is good in tomato-based recipes, and with roasted vegetables, lentils, and beans. It is also an essential ingredient in a bouquet garni. Thyme aids the digestion of fatty foods and works as a powerful antiseptic.

TARRAGON

A popular herb in French cooking, tarragon has an affinity with all egg- and cheese-based dishes. The short, slender-leaf French variety has a warm, aniseed flavor and is considered to be superior to Russian tarragon. Tarragon has diuretic properties and can relieve indigestion. Infused in a herbal tisane, it can soothe sore throats and promote restful sleep.

Buying and Storing: Fresh herbs are widely available, sold loose, in packets, or growing in pots. The packets do not keep for long and should be stored in the fridge. Place stems of fresh herbs in a half-filled jar of water and cover with a plastic bag. Sealed with a rubber band, the herbs should keep in the fridge for a week. Growing herbs should be kept on a sunny windowsill. If watered regularly, and not cut too often, they will keep for months.

Drying Herbs

Bay, rosemary, sage, thyme, and marjoram all dry well, but other more delicate herbs, such as basil, cilantro, and parsley are better used fresh. Pick herbs before they flower, preferably on a sunny morning after the dew has dried. Avoid washing them—instead brush with a pastry brush or wipe with a dry cloth. Tie the herbs in bunches and hang them upside down in a warm, dark place. The leaves should be dry and crisp after a week. Leave the herbs in bundles or strip the leaves from the stems and store in airtight jars.

Making Herbal Infusions

Infusions, or tisanes, are made from steeping fresh herbs in boiling water. They can be used as a medicinal gargle or refreshing healthy drink. Peppermint tea is an excellent remedy for indigestion or irritable bowel syndrome and is best drunk after a meal.

To make peppermint tea: pour boiling water over fresh peppermint leaves. Cover the bowl and leave to stand for about 10 minutes, then strain the liquid into a cup and drink.

Tarragon

Sprouted Seeds, Pulses, and Grains

Sprouts are quite remarkable in terms of nutritional content. Once the seed (or pulse, or grain) has germinated, the nutritional value rises dramatically. There are almost 30 percent more B vitamins and 60 percent more vitamin C in the sprout than in the seed, pulse, or grain. Supermarkets and health food stores sell a variety of sprouts, but to grow them at home all you need is a jar, some cheesecloth, and a rubber band.

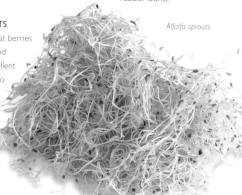

Alfalfa sprouts

MUNG BEAN SPROUTS

The most commonly available bean sprouts, these are popular in Chinese and Asian cooking, where they are used in soups, salads, and stir-fries. They are fairly large, with a crunchy texture and a delicate flavor.

ALFALFA SPROUTS

These tiny, wispy white sprouts have a mild, nutty flavor. They are best eaten raw to retain their crunchy texture.

WHEAT BERRY SPROUTS

Sprouts grown from wheat berries have a crunchy texture and sweet flavor, and are excellent in breads. If they are left to grow, the sprouts will become wheatgrass, a powerful detoxifier that is usually made into a juice.

Mung bean sprouts

GARBANZO BEAN SPROUTS

Sprouts grown from garbanzos have a nutty flavor and add substance to dishes.

LENTIL SPROUTS

These sprouts have a slightly spicy, peppery flavor and thin, white shoots. Use only whole lentils: split ones won't sprout.

ADZUKI BEAN SPROUTS

These fine wispy sprouts have a sweet nutty taste. Use in salads and stir-fries.

Sprouting Seeds, Pulses, and Grains

Larger pulses, such as garbanzo beans, take longer to sprout than small beans, but they are all easy to grow and are usually ready to eat in three or four days. Store sprouts in a covered container in the fridge for 2–3 days.

2 The next day, pour away the water through the cheesecloth and fill the jar with water again. Shake gently, then turn the jar upside down, and drain thoroughly. Leave the jar on its side in a warm place, away from direct sunlight.

1 Wash 3 tablespoons seeds, pulses, or grains thoroughly in water, then place in a large jar. Fill the jar with lukewarm water, cover with a piece of cheesecloth, and fasten securely with a rubber band. Let stand in a warm place overnight.

3 Rinse the seeds, pulses or grains three times a day, until they have grown to the desired size. Make sure they are drained thoroughly to prevent them turning rancid. Remove from the jar, rinse well, and remove any ungerminated beans.

How to Use Bean Sprouts

• Sprouted pulses and beans have a denser more fibrous texture, while sprouts grown from seeds are lighter. Use a mixture of the three for a variety of tastes and textures.

• Mung bean sprouts are often used in Asian food, particularly stir-fries, and require little cooking.

• Alfalfa sprouts are good as part of a sandwich filling as well as in salads. They are not suited to cooking.

• Sprouted grains are good in breads, adding a pleasant crunchy texture. Knead them in after the first rising, before shaping the loaf.

• Use garbanzo bean and lentil sprouts in casseroles and bakes.

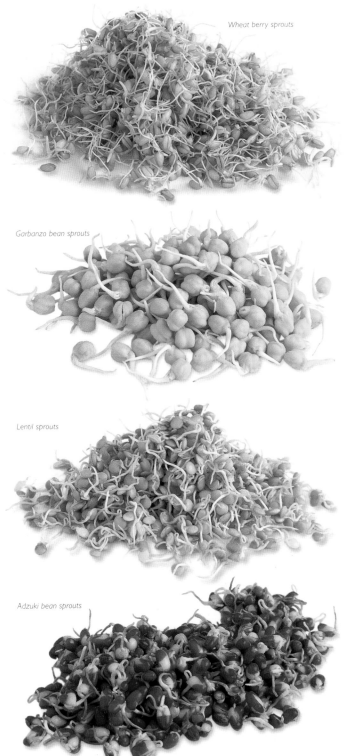

Wheat berry sprouts

Garbanzo bean sprouts

Lentil sprouts

Adzuki bean sprouts

Buying and Storing: If you can, choose fresh, crisp sprouts with the seed or bean still attached. Avoid any that are slimy or musty-looking. Sprouts are best eaten on the day they are bought, but if fresh they will keep, wrapped in a plastic bag in the fridge, for 2–3 days. Rinse and pat dry before use.

Health Benefits: Sprouted seeds, pulses, and grains supply rich amounts of protein, B complex vitamins, and vitamins C and E, potassium, and phosphorus which, due to the sprouting process, are in an easily digestible form. In Chinese medicine, sprouts are highly valued for their ability to cleanse and rejuvenate the system.

Tips on Sprouting

• Use whole seeds and beans, as split ones will not germinate.

• Regular rinsing with fresh water and draining is essential when sprouting to prevent the beans from turning rancid and moldy.

• Cover the sprouting jar with cheesecloth to allow air to circulate and to let water in and out.

• After two or three days, the jar can be placed in sunlight to encourage the green pigment chlorophyll and increase the sprout's magnesium and fiber content.

• Soybean and garbanzo bean sprouts need to be rinsed four times a day.

• Keen sprouters may wish to invest in a special sprouting container that comes with draining trays.

Sprouting container

Sea Vegetables

The West has only relatively recently acknowledged the extraordinary variety and remarkable health benefits of sea vegetables, which have been an essential part of the Asian diet for centuries. Sea vegetables are highly versatile and can be used as the main component of a dish, to add texture and substance, or as a seasoning. Some sea vegetables, such as wakame, hijiki, and kombu (or kelp), can be used in soups, stews, and stir-fries, while others, such as agar-agar and carrageen, are used as a setting agent in molds, mousses, and cheesecakes.

Laver

NORI

This useful sea vegetable has a delicate texture and mild flavor. It is sold in thin purple-black sheets, which turn a pretty, translucent green when toasted or cooked. It is one of the few sea vegetables that does not require soaking. Nori is processed by being chopped, flattened, and dried on frames, like paper. In Japanese cooking, the sheets are used to wrap delicate, small packages of vinegared rice and vegetables that are eaten as sushi. Once toasted and crisp, nori is crumbled and used as a garnish.

LAVER

A relation of nori, which grows outside Japan, laver is commonly found around the shores of Britain. Unlike Japanese nori, it is not cultivated. Laver is used in traditional regional cooking—particularly in Wales, Scotland, and Ireland. It is cooked into a thick dark purée, which can be spread on hot toast or mixed with oatmeal to make the Welsh delicacy, laverbread. It can also be added to sauces and stuffings. Available ready-cooked in cans from health food stores, laver has a stronger flavor than nori and a higher concentration of vitamins and minerals.

Nori sheets and flakes

Toasting Nori

Nori can be toasted over a burner until it is very crisp. The sheets can then be crumbled between the fingers and used as a garnish for soups, salads, or stir-fries. Take care when you are toasting the nori sheets that you do not scorch them—or your fingers.

1 Hold a sheet of nori with a pair of tongs about 2 inches above a warm burner for about 1 minute, moving it around so it toasts evenly and turns bright green and crisp.

2 Leave the nori sheet to cool for a few moments, then crumble. Sprinkle over salad, or use to garnish soups or stir-fries.

Arame

color from brown to a delicate green. Wakame has a mild flavor and is one of the most versatile sea vegetables. Soak briefly and use in salads and soups, or toast, crumble, and use as a condiment. It is rich in calcium and vitamins B and C.

KOMBU

Known as kelp in the West, kombu is now farmed. It is a brown sea vegetable and is usually sold dried in strips, although in Japan it is available in a multitude of forms. It has a very strong flavor and is used in slowly cooked dishes, soups, and stocks—it is an essential ingredient in the Japanese stock, dashi. A small strip of kombu added to beans while they are cooking will soften them and increase their digestibility, as well as their nutritional value. Kombu is richer in iodine than other sea vegetables, and also contains calcium, potassium, and iron.

ARAME

Sold in delicate, black strips, arame has a mild, slightly sweet flavor. If you haven't tried sea vegetables before, it is a good one to start with. It needs to be soaked before using in stir-fries or salads, but if using in moist or slow-cooked dishes, such as noodles and soups, it can be added straight from the packet. Arame has been used to treat female disorders and is recommended for high blood pressure. It is rich in iodine, calcium, and iron.

WAKAME

This sea vegetable is often confused with its relative, kombu, because it looks very similar until it is soaked, when it changes

Kombu or kelp

Preparing Arame

Soaking and cooking times vary depending on how the arame is to be used.

1 Rinse the arame in a strainer under cold, running water, then place in a bowl and cover with cold water. Leave to soak for 5 minutes—it should double in volume. Drain and place in a saucepan.

2 Add fresh water and bring to a boil. Simmer for 20 minutes until tender.

Wakame

Hijiki

HIJIKI

This sea vegetable looks similar to arame, but is thicker and has a slightly stronger flavor. Once soaked, hijiki can be sautéed or added to soups and salads, but it does require longer cooking than most sea vegetables. It expands considerably during soaking, so only a small amount is needed. It is particularly rich in calcium and iron.

Using Agar-agar to Make Jelly

Agar-agar can be used in place of gelatin; ¼oz agar-agar flakes will set about 2½ cups liquid.

1 Place ¼oz agar-agar flakes in a saucepan with 1¼ cups cold water; let soak for 15 minutes.

2 Bring to a boil, then simmer for a few minutes, until the flakes dissolve. Stir in 1¼ cups fresh orange juice. Pour into a mold and set aside to cool, then chill in the fridge until set.

DULSE

A purple-red sea vegetable, dulse has flat fronds, which have a chewy texture and spicy flavor when cooked. For hundreds of years, dulse was popular in North America and northern Europe and was traded on both sides of the Atlantic. It needs to be soaked until soft before adding to salads, noodle dishes, soups, and vegetable dishes. It can also be toasted and crumbled to make a nourishing garnish.

Dulse is rich in several minerals—potassium, iodine, phosphorus, iron, and manganese.

AGAR-AGAR

The vegetarian equivalent to the animal-derived gelatin, agar-agar can be used as a setting agent in both sweet and non-sweet dishes. Known as kanten in Japan, it can be bought as flakes or strands, both of which need to be dissolved in water before use. Agar-agar has a neutral taste and its gelling abilities vary according to the other ingredients in a dish, so you may need to experiment, if substituting it for gelatin in a recipe, to achieve the best results. It is more effective than gelatin, so only a small amount is needed. It is said to be an effective laxative.

Dulse

Carrageen (left) and agar-agar flakes

CARRAGEEN

This fern-like seaweed, also known as Irish moss, is found along the Atlantic coasts of America and Europe. Like agar-agar, it has gelling properties, but produces a softer set, making it useful for molds and mousses and as a thickener in soups and stews. It is used for treating colds and bronchial problems as well as digestive disorders.

Buying and Storing: Sea vegetables are usually sold dried and will keep for months. Once the packet is opened, transfer the sea vegetables to an airtight jar. Fresh sea vegetables may be stored in the fridge, but will remain fresh for only 1–2 days. Rinse well before use.

Health Benefits: The health benefits of sea vegetables have been recognized for centuries and range from improving the luster of hair and clarity of the skin to reducing cholesterol levels in the body. Sea vegetables are particularly rich in the antioxidant beta carotene. They contain some of the B complex vitamins, and significant amounts of the major minerals, such as calcium, magnesium, potassium, phosphorus, and iron, as well as useful amounts of trace elements, such as selenium, zinc, and iodine.

The rich mineral content of sea vegetables benefits the nervous system, helping to reduce stress. It also boosts the immune system, aiding the metabolism, while the iodine content prevents goiter and helps thyroid function. Research shows that alginic acid found in some seaweeds, notably kombu, arame, hijiki, and wakame, binds with heavy metals, such as cadmium, lead, mercury, and radium, in our intestines and helps to eliminate them.

COOK'S TIP

Some sea vegetables simply need washing and soaking for a few minutes before serving or adding to dishes; others require prolonged soaking and cooking before they are tender enough to eat. Most expand considerably after soaking, so only a small amount is required.

Rolled Sushi with Mixed Filling

INGREDIENTS
1 ½ cups sushi rice
4 sheets nori seaweed, for rolling
soy sauce and gari (ginger pickles),
    to serve

FOR THE MIXED VINEGAR
8 teaspoons rice vinegar
4 ½ teaspoons sugar
⅔ teaspoon sea salt

FOR THE FILLING
4 large dried shiitake mushrooms
7 ½ teaspoons soy sauce
1 tablespoon each of mirin, sake or dry
    white wine, and sugar
1 small carrot, quartered lengthwise
½ cucumber, quartered lengthwise,
    seeds removed

Makes 32 pieces

1 Cook the rice in salted boiling water, then drain. Meanwhile, heat the ingredients for the mixed vinegar. Let the vinegar cool, then add to the hot cooked rice. Stir well with a spatula, fanning the rice constantly—this gives the rice an attractive glaze. Cover with a damp cloth and let cool. Do not put in the fridge, as this will make the rice harden.

2 To make the filling, soak the dried shiitake mushrooms in scant 1 cup water for 30 minutes; drain, reserving the soaking water, and remove their stems. Pour the reserved soaking water into a saucepan and add the remaining filling ingredients (except the cucumber), then simmer for 4–5 minutes. Remove the carrot and set aside. Continue cooking until all the liquid has evaporated, then thinly slice the shiitake mushrooms and set aside for the filling.

3 Place a bamboo mat (makisu) on a chopping board. Lay a sheet of nori, shiny side down, on the mat.

4 Spread a quarter of the prepared, dressed rice over the nori, using your fingers to press it down evenly. Leave a ½ -inch space at the top and bottom. Place a quarter of each of the filling ingredients—the sliced mushrooms, carrot, and cucumber—across the middle of the layer of rice.

5 Carefully hold the nearest edge of the nori and the mat, then roll up the nori using the mat as a guide to make a neat tube of rice with the filling ingredients in the middle. Roll the rice tightly to ensure that the grains stick together and to keep the filling in place. Roll the sushi off the mat and make three more rolls in the same way.

6 Using a wet knife, cut each roll into eight pieces and stand them upright on a platter. Wipe the blade and rinse it under cold water between cuts to prevent the rice from sticking. Serve soy sauce and gari with the sushi.

Cereal Grains

Grains have been cultivated throughout the world for centuries. The seeds of cereal grasses, they are packed with concentrated goodness and are an important source of complex carbohydrates, protein, vitamins, and minerals. The most popular types of grain, such as wheat, rice, oats, barley, and corn or maize, come in various forms, from whole grains to flours. Inexpensive and readily available, grains are incredibly versatile and should form a major part of our diet.

Wheat

Wheat is the largest and most important grain crop in the world and has been cultivated since 7,000 BC.

The wheat kernel comprises three parts: bran, germ, and endosperm. Wheat bran is the outer husk, while wheat germ is the nutritious seed from which the plant grows. Sprouted wheat is an excellent food, highly recommended in cancer prevention diets. The endosperm, the inner part of the kernel, is full of starch and protein and forms the basis of wheat flour. In addition to flour, wheat comes in various other forms.

Wholewheat berries

Wheatgrass

WHEAT BERRIES

These are whole wheat grains with the husks removed and they can be bought in health food stores. Wheat berries may be used to add a sweet, nutty flavor and chewy texture to breads, soups, and stews, or can be combined with rice or other grains. Wheat berries must be soaked overnight, then cooked in boiling salted water until tender. If they are left to germinate, the berries sprout into wheatgrass, a powerful detoxifier and cleanser (see below).

WHEAT BRAN

Wheat bran is the outer husk of the wheat kernel and is a by-product of white flour production. It is very high in soluble dietary fiber, which makes it nature's most effective laxative. Wheat bran makes a healthy addition to bread doughs, breakfast cereals, cakes, muffins, and cookies, and it can also be used to add substance to stews and bakes.

Wheatgrass—a Natural Healer

Grown from the wholewheat grain, wheatgrass has been recognized for centuries for its general healing qualities. When juiced, it is a powerful detoxifier and cleanser and is a rich source of B vitamins and vitamins A, C, and E, as well as all the known minerals. Its vibrant green color comes from chlorophyl (known as "nature's healer"), which works directly on the liver to eliminate harmful toxins. It is also reputed to have anti-aging capabilities.

Once it is juiced, wheatgrass must be consumed within 15 minutes, preferably on an empty stomach. Some people may experience nausea or dizziness when drinking the juice for the first time, but this will soon disappear.

Wheat germ

Wheat flakes

Bulgur wheat

way as wheat berries (although it cooks in less time), or as an alternative to rice and other grains. When cooked, it has a slightly sticky texture and pleasant crunchiness. Serve it as an accompaniment, or use in salads and pilaffs.

BULGUR WHEAT

Unlike cracked wheat, this grain is made from cooked wheat berries, which have the bran removed, and are then dried and crushed. This light, nutty grain is simply soaked in water for 20 minutes, then drained—some manufacturers specify cold water, but boiling water produces a softer grain. It can also be cooked in boiling water until tender. Bulgur wheat is the main ingredient in the Middle Eastern salad, tabbouleh, where it is combined with chopped parsley, mint, tomatoes, cucumber, and onion, and dressed with lemon juice and olive oil.

Cooking Wheat Berries

Wheat berries make a delicious addition to salads, and they can also be used to add texture to breads and stews.

Place the wheat berries in a bowl and cover with cold water. Soak overnight, then rinse thoroughly and drain.

2 Place the wheat berries in a pan with water. Bring to a boil, then cover, and simmer for 1–2 hours, until tender, replenishing with water when necessary.

WHEAT FLAKES

Steamed and softened berries that have been rolled and pressed are known as wheat flakes or rolled wheat. They are best used on their own or mixed with other flaked grains in porridge, as a base for muesli, or to add nutrients and substance to breads and cakes.

WHEAT GERM

The nutritious heart of the whole wheat berry, wheat germ is a rich source of protein, vitamins B and E, and iron. It is used in much the same way as wheat bran and lends a pleasant, nutty flavor to breakfast cereals and porridge. It is available toasted or untoasted. Store wheat germ in an airtight container in the fridge as it can become rancid if kept at room temperature.

CRACKED WHEAT

This is made from crushed wheat berries and retains all the nutrients of wholewheat. Often confused with bulgur wheat, cracked wheat can be used in the same

SEMOLINA

Made from the endosperm of durum
wheat, semolina can be used to make a
hot milk pudding or it can be added to
cakes, cookies, and breads to give them a
pleasant grainy texture.

COUSCOUS

Although this looks like a grain, couscous
is a form of pasta made by steaming and
drying cracked durum wheat. Couscous is
popular in North Africa, where it forms
the basis of a national dish of the same
name. Individual grains are moistened by
hand, passed through a strainer, and then
steamed in a couscousière, suspended
over a bubbling vegetable stew, until light

Semolina

Cooking Couscous

Traditionally, the preparation of couscous
is a time-consuming business, requiring
lengthy steaming. The couscous found in
most stores nowadays, however, is
precooked, which cuts the preparation
time drastically.

1 Place the couscous in a large bowl, add
enough boiling water to cover and
leave for 10 minutes, or until all the water
has been absorbed. Separate the grains,
season and mix in a pat of butter.

2 Alternatively, moisten the grains and
place in a cheesecloth-lined steamer.
Steam for 15 minutes, or until the grains
are tender and fluffy.

and fluffy. Nowadays, the couscous that is
generally available is the quick-cooking
variety, which simply needs soaking,
although it can also be steamed or baked.
Couscous has a fairly bland flavor, which
makes it a good foil for spicy dishes.

WHEAT FLOUR

This is ground from the whole grain and
may be whole wheat or white, depending
on the degree of processing. Stone-
ground flour is high in a protein called
gluten, which makes it ideal for bread
making, while soft flour is lower in gluten
but higher in starch and is better for light

cakes and pastries. Durum wheat flour
comes from one of the hardest varieties
of wheat and is used to make pasta. Most
commercial white flour is a combination
of soft and hard wheat, which produces an
all-purpose flour.

Because the refining process robs many
commercial flours of most of their
nutrients, the lost vitamins and minerals
are synthetically replaced. When buying
flour, look for brands that are unbleached
and organically produced, as these have
fewer chemical additives. Nutritionally,
stone-ground whole wheat flour is the
best buy because it is largely unprocessed

Couscous

Wheat flour (left) and malted brown flour, which contains flour from malted wheat grains. Stone-ground versions are available

and retains all the valuable nutrients. It produces slightly heavier breads, cakes, and pastries than white flour, but can be combined with white flour to make lighter versions, although, of course, the nutritional value will not be so high.

SEITAN

Used as a meat replacement, seitan is made from wheat gluten and has a firm, chewy texture. It can be found in the chiller cabinet of health food stores. Seitan has a neutral flavor that benefits from marinating. Slice or cut into chunks and stir-fry, or add to stews and pasta sauces during the last few minutes of cooking time. Seitan does not need to be cooked for long, just heated through.

Buying and Storing: Buy wheat-based foods from stores with a high turnover of stock. Wheat berries can be kept for around 6 months, but whole wheat flour should be used within 3 months, as its oils turn rancid. Always decant grains into airtight containers and store in a cool, dark place. Wheat germ deteriorates very quickly at room temperature and should be stored in an airtight container in the fridge for no more than a month.

Health Benefits: Wheat is most nutritious when it is unprocessed and in its whole form. (When milled into white flour, wheat loses a staggering 80 percent of its nutrients.) Wheat is an excellent source of dietary fiber, the B vitamins, and vitamin E, as well as iron, selenium, and zinc. Fiber is the most discussed virtue of whole wheat and most of this is concentrated in the bran. Eating one or more spoonfuls of bran a day is recommended to relieve constipation. Numerous studies show fiber to be effective in inhibiting colon and rectal cancer, varicose veins, hemorrhoids, and obesity. Phytoestrogens found in wholegrains may also ward off breast cancer. On the negative side, wheat is also a well-known allergen and triggers celiac disease, a gluten intolerance.

Seitan

Rice

Throughout Asia, a meal is considered incomplete without rice. It is a staple food for over half the world's population, and almost every culture has its own repertoire of rice dishes, ranging from risottos to pilaffs. What's more, this valuable food provides a good source of vitamins and minerals, as well as a steady supply of energy.

White and brown long grain rice

Jasmine fragrant rice

LONG GRAIN RICE

The most widely used type of rice is long grain rice, where the grain is five times as long as it is wide. Long grain brown rice has had its outer husk removed, leaving the bran and germ intact, which gives it a chewy nutty flavor. It takes longer to cook than white rice, but contains more fiber, vitamins, and minerals. Long grain white rice has had its husk, bran, and germ removed, taking most of the nutrients with them, and leaving a bland-flavored rice that is light and fluffy when cooked. It is often whitened with chalk, talc, or other preservatives, so rinsing is essential. Easy-cook long grain white rice, sometimes called parboiled or converted rice, has been steamed under pressure. This process hardens the grain and makes it difficult to overcook, and some nutrients are transferred from the bran and germ into the kernel during this process. Easy-cook brown rice cooks more quickly than normal brown rice.

JASMINE RICE

This rice has a soft, sticky texture and a delicious, mildly perfumed flavor—which accounts for its other name, fragrant rice. It is a long grain rice that is widely used in Thai cooking, where its delicate flavor tempers strongly spiced food.

Cooking Long Grain Brown Rice

There are many methods and opinions on how to cook rice. The absorption method is one of the simplest and retains valuable nutrients, which would otherwise be lost in cooking water that is drained away.

Different types of rice have different powers of absorption, however the general rule of thumb for long grain rice is to use double the quantity of water to rice. For example, use 1 cup of rice to 2 cups of water. 1 cup long grain rice is sufficient for about four people as an accompanying side dish.

1 Rinse the rice in a strainer under cold, running water. Place in a heavy-based saucepan and add the measured cold water. Bring to a boil, uncovered, then reduce the heat, and stir the rice. Add salt to taste, if you wish.

2 Cover the pan with a tight-fitting lid. Simmer for 25–35 minutes, without removing the lid, until the water is absorbed and the rice tender. Remove from the heat and let stand, covered, for 5 minutes before serving.

Red rice

Wild rice

RED RICE

This rice comes from the Camargue in France and has a distinctive chewy texture and a nutty flavor. It is an unusually hard grain, which although it takes about an hour to cook, retains its shape. Cooking intensifies its red color, making it a distinctive addition to salads and stuffings.

WILD RICE

This is not a true rice, but an aquatic grass grown in North America. It has dramatic, long, slender brown-black grains that have a nutty flavor and chewy texture. It takes longer to cook than most types of rice—35–60 minutes, depending on whether you like it chewy or tender—but you can reduce the cooking time by soaking it in water overnight. Wild rice is extremely nutritious. It contains all eight essential amino acids and is particularly rich in lysine. It is a good source of fiber, low in calories, and gluten free. Use in stuffings, serve plain, or mix with other rices in pilaffs and rice salads.

BASMATI RICE

This is a slender, long grain rice, which is grown in the foothills of the Himalayas. It is aged for a year after harvest, giving it a characteristic light, fluffy texture and aromatic flavor. Its name means "fragrant."

Both white and brown types of basmati rice are available. Brown basmati contains more nutrients, and has a slightly nuttier flavor than the white variety. Widely used in Indian cooking, basmati rice has a cooling effect on hot and spicy curries. It is also excellent for biryanis and for rice salads, when you want very light, fluffy separate grains.

White and brown basmati rice

Quick Ways to Flavor Rice

• Cook brown rice in vegetable stock with sliced dried apricots. Sauté an onion in a little oil and add ground cumin, coriander, and fresh chopped chile, then mix in the cooked rice.

• Add raisins and toasted almonds to saffron-infused rice.

Valencia rice

• When making risotto, replace a quarter of the vegetable stock with red or white wine.

• Add a bay leaf, the juice and zest of a lemon, or a lemon grass stalk, and cardamom pods to the cooking water.
• Saffron adds a yellow color to risotto rice. Add a few strands to the vegetable stock.

VALENCIA RICE

Traditionally used for making Spanish paella, this short grain rice is not as sturdy as risotto rice and needs to be handled with care because it breaks down easily. The best way of cooking paella is to leave the rice unstirred once all the ingredients are in the pan.

RISOTTO RICE

To make Italian risotto, it is essential that you use a special, fat, short grain rice. Arborio rice, which originates from the Po Valley region in Italy, is the most widely sold variety of risotto rice, but you may also find varieties such as Carnaroli and Vialone Nano in specialty stores. When cooked, most rice absorbs around three times its weight in water; risotto rice can absorb nearly five times its weight, and the result is a creamy grain that still retains a slight bite.

Above, clockwise from left: Arborio, carnaroli, and vialone nano risotto rice

Making a Simple Risotto

A good risotto, which is creamy and moist with tender grains that retain a slight bite, is easy to make. The secrets are to use the correct type of rice (arborio, carnaroli, or vialone nano); to add the cooking liquid gradually—it should be completely absorbed by the rice before the next ladleful is added; and to stir the risotto frequently to prevent the grains from sticking.

INGREDIENTS

1 tablespoon olive oil
small pat of butter
1 onion, finely chopped (½ cup)
1¾ cups risotto rice
5 cups hot vegetable stock
⅔ cup freshly grated
   Parmesan cheese
salt and freshly ground black pepper

SERVES 4

Variations

• Add finely chopped cooked (not pickled) beet toward the end of the cooking time to give the rice a vibrant pink color and slight sweetness.

• To make mushroom and broccoli risotto, sauté 2 cups sliced or chopped flat mushrooms with the onion. Blanch 2 cups broccoli flowerets for 3 minutes, until tender, and add toward the end of cooking time.

1 Heat the oil and butter in a large, heavy-based pan, then cook the onion for 7 minutes, until soft, stirring occasionally. Add the rice and stir to coat the grains in the hot oil and butter.

2 Add a quarter of the stock and cook over low to medium heat, stirring frequently, until the liquid is absorbed. Add more stock, a little at a time, stirring, until all the liquid is added and absorbed.

3 After about 20 minutes, the grains will be creamy, but still retain a bite. Turn off the heat, stir in the Parmesan, and check the seasoning. Add salt and pepper to taste and serve immediately.

Japanese Rice Products

The Japanese are extremely resourceful when it comes to exploiting the vast potential of rice.

Sake This spirit is Japan's national drink; it can also be used in cooking.

Mirin Sweet rice wine that is delicious in marinades and non-sweet dishes, and is a key ingredient in teriyaki.

Rice vinegar Popular throughout Asia, this ranges in color from white to brown. Japanese rice vinegar has a mild, mellow flavor. The Chinese version is much harsher.

Amasake A healthful rice drink made by adding enzymes from fermented rice to wholegrain pudding rice. It has a similar consistency to soy "milk" and can be flavored. Amasake may be used for baking or to make creamy desserts. It is also an excellent and easily digestible weaning food.

Right, clockwise from top left: amasake, mirin, rice vinegar, and sake.

PUDDING RICE

This rounded, short grain rice is suitable for milk puddings and rice desserts. The grains swell and absorb a great deal of milk during cooking, which gives the pudding a soft, creamy consistency. Brown pudding rice is also available.

GLUTINOUS RICE

This rice is almost round in shape and has a slightly sweet flavor. Despite its name, the rice is gluten-free. The grains stick together when cooked owing to their high starch content, making the rice easier to eat with chopsticks.

Glutinous rice, which can be either white, black, or purple, is used in many Southeast Asian countries to make sticky, creamy puddings. In China, white glutinous rice is often wrapped in lotus leaves and steamed to make a popular dim sum dish.

Pudding rice

White and black glutinous rice

JAPANESE SUSHI RICE

Similar to glutinous rice, this is mixed with rice vinegar to make sushi. Most sushi rice eaten in the West is grown in California.

Buying and Storing: To ensure freshness, always buy rice from stores that have a regular turnover of stock. Store in an airtight container in a cool, dry, dark place to keep out moisture and insects. Wash before use to remove any impurities. Cooked rice should be cooled quickly, then chilled, and reheated thoroughly before serving.

Health Benefits: Rice is a valuable source of complex carbohydrates and fiber. In its whole form, it is a good source of B vitamins. White rice is deprived of much of its nutrients because the bran and germ have been removed. The starch in rice is absorbed slowly, keeping blood-sugar levels on an even keel and making it an important food for diabetics. Research shows that rice may benefit sufferers of psoriasis. It can also be used to

Sushi rice

treat digestive disorders, calm the nervous system, prevent kidney stones, and reduce the risk of bowel cancer. However, the phytates found in brown rice can inhibit the absorption of iron and calcium.

Quick Ideas for Rice

Rice can be served plain, but it is also good in one-dish meals, marrying well with a host of exotic flavorings and simple storecupboard ingredients.
• To make a Middle-Eastern inspired rice dish, cook long grain brown rice in vegetable stock, then stir in some toasted slivered almonds, pieces of dried date and fig, cooked garbanzo beans, and chopped fresh mint.
• For a simple pullao, gently fry a finely chopped onion in sunflower oil with cardamom pods, a cinnamon stick, and cloves, then stir in basmati rice. Add water, infused with a pinch of saffron, and cook until tender. Toward the end of the cooking time, add golden raisins and cashew nuts, then garnish with chopped cilantro.

Rice Products

Rice flakes These are made by steaming and rolling whole or white grains. They are light and quick-cooking, and can be added raw to muesli or used to make porridge, creamy puddings, bread, cookies, and cakes.

Rice bran Like wheat and oat bran, rice bran comes from the husk of the grain kernel. It is high in soluble dietary fiber and useful for adding texture and substance to bread, cakes and cookies, and stews.

Rice flour Often used to make sticky Asian cakes and sweets, rice flour can also be used to thicken sauces. Because rice flour does not contain gluten, cakes made with it are rather flat. It can be combined with wheat flour to make cakes and bread, but produces a crumbly loaf. Rice powder is a very fine rice flour, found in Asian stores.

Right, clockwise from top left: rice bran, rice flour, rice powder, and rice flakes.

Other Grains

Wheat and rice are undoubtedly the most widely used grains, yet there are others, such as oats, rye, corn, barley, quinoa, and spelt, that should not be ignored because they provide variety in our diet and are packed with nutrients. Grains come in many forms, from whole grains to flour, and are used for baking, breakfast cereals, and cooked dishes.

OATS

Available rolled, flaked, as oatmeal, or oatbran, oats are warming and sustaining when cooked. Like rye, oats are a popular grain in northern Europe, particularly Scotland, where they are commonly turned into hot oatmeal, oatcakes, and pancakes.

Whole oats are unprocessed with the nutritious bran and germ remaining intact. Oat groats are the hulled, whole kernel, while rolled oats are made from groats that have been heated and pressed flat. Quick-cooking rolled oats have been precooked in water and then dried, which diminishes their nutritional value. Medium oatmeal is best in cakes and breads, while fine is ideal in pancakes, and fruit and milk drinks. Oat flour is gluten-free and has to be mixed with other flours that contain gluten to make leavened bread. Oat bran can be sprinkled over breakfast cereals and mixed into any kind of yogurt.

Health Benefits: Oats are perhaps the most nutritious of all the grains. Recent research has focused on the ability of oat bran to reduce blood cholesterol (sometimes with dramatic results), while beneficial HDL cholesterol levels increase. For best results, oat bran should be eaten daily at regular intervals.

High in fiber, oats are an effective laxative and also feature protease inhibitors, a combination that has been found to inhibit certain cancers. Oats also contain vitamin E and some B vitamins, as well as iron, calcium, magnesium, phosphorus, and potassium.

Below, clockwise from top left: Rolled oats, oatmeal, whole oats and oat bran

Rye: grain and flour

RYE

The most popular grain for bread-making in Eastern Europe, Scandinavia, and Russia, rye flour produces a dark, dense, and dry loaf that keeps well. It is a hardy grain, which grows where most others fail—hence its popularity in colder climates. Rye is low in gluten and so rye flour is often mixed with high-gluten wheat flours to create lighter textured breads, the color of which is sometimes intensified using molasses. The whole grain can be soaked overnight, then cooked in boiling water until tender, but the flour, with its robust, full flavor and grayish color, is the most commonly used form. The flour ranges from dark to light, depending on whether the bran and germ have been removed.

Health Benefits: Rye is a good source of vitamin E and some B vitamins, as well as protein, calcium, iron, phosphorus, and potassium. It is also high in fiber, and is used in natural medicine to help to strengthen the digestive system.

CORN

Although we are most familiar with yellow corn or maize, blue, red, black, and even multicolored varieties can also be found. It is an essential storecupboard ingredient in the United States, the Caribbean, and Italy, and comes in many forms.

Masa harina

Maize meal, or masa harina, is made from the cooked whole grain, which is ground into flour and commonly used to make the Mexican flat bread, tortilla.

Cornmeal

The main culinary uses for cornmeal are cornbread, a classic, southern American bread, and polenta, which confusingly is both the Italian name for cornmeal as well as a dish made with the grain. Polenta (the cooked dish) is a thick, golden dish, which is often flavored with butter and cheese

Making Polenta

Polenta makes an excellent alternative to mashed potato. It needs plenty of seasoning and is even better with a pat of butter and cheese, such as Parmesan, Gorgonzola, or Taleggio. Serve with stews or casseroles.

1 Pour 4 cups water into a heavy-based saucepan and bring to a boil. Remove from the heat.

2 In a steady stream, gradually add 1½ cups instant polenta and mix constantly with a balloon whisk to avoid any lumps forming.

3 Return the pan to the heat and cook, stirring continuously with a wooden spoon, until the polenta is thick and creamy and starts to come away from the sides of the pan—this will take only a few minutes if you are using instant polenta.

4 Season to taste with salt and plenty of ground black pepper, then add a generous pat of butter and mix well. Remove from the heat and stir in the cheese, if using.

Clockwise from top left: Blue and yellow cornmeal, cornstarch, popcorn, masa harina, and polenta.

or chopped herbs. Once cooked, polenta can also be left to cool, then cut into slabs and fried, grilled, or griddled until golden brown. It is delicious with roasted vegetables. Ready-to-slice polenta is available from some supermarkets.

Polenta grain comes in various grades, ranging from fine to coarse. You can buy polenta that takes 40–45 minutes to cook or an "instant" part-cooked version that can be cooked in less than 5 minutes.

In the Caribbean, cornmeal is used to make puddings and dumplings.

Cornstarch

This fine white powder is a useful thickening agent for sauces, soups, and casseroles. It can also be added to cakes.

Hominy

These are the husked whole grains of corn. They should be cooked in boiling water until softened, then used in stews and soups, or added to cakes and muffins.

Grits

Coarsely ground, dried yellow or white corn is known as grits. Use for pancakes or add to baked goods.

Popcorn

This is a separate strain of corn that is grown specifically to make the popular snack food. The kernel's hard outer casing explodes when heated.

Quinoa

Popcorn can easily be made at home and flavored sweet or non-sweet according to taste. The store-bought types are often high in salt or sugar.

Health Benefits: In American folk medicine, corn is considered a diuretic and a mild stimulant. Corn is said to prevent cancer of the colon, breast, and prostate and to lower the risk of heart disease. It is believed to be the only grain that contains vitamin A as well as some of the B vitamins and iron.

BARLEY

Believed to be the oldest cultivated grain, barley is still a fundamental part of the everyday diet in Eastern Europe, the Middle East, and Asia.

Pearl barley, the most usual form, is husked, steamed, and then polished to give it its characteristic ivory-colored appearance. It has a mild, sweet flavor and chewy texture, and can be added to soups, stews, and bakes. It is also used to make old-fashioned barley water.

Pot barley is the whole grain with just the inedible outer husk removed. It takes much longer to cook than pearl barley.

Barley flakes, which make a satisfying breakfast dish, and barley flour are also available.

Health Benefits: Pot barley is more nutritious than pearl barley because it contains extra fiber, calcium, phosphorus, iron, magnesium, and B vitamins. Barley was once used to increase potency and boost physical strength. More recently, studies have shown that its fiber content may help to prevent constipation and other digestive problems, as well as heart disease and certain cancers. In addition, the protease inhibitors in barley have been found to suppress cancer of the intestines, and eating barley regularly may also reduce the amount of harmful cholesterol produced by the liver.

Clockwise from left: Pot barley, barley flakes, and pearl barley

Lemon Barley Water

INGREDIENTS

1 cup pearl barley (8 ounces)
7¹/₂ cups water
grated rind of 1 lemon
¹/₄ cup golden superfine sugar (2 ounces)
juice of 2 lemons

1 Rinse the barley, then place in a large saucepan and cover with the water. Bring to a boil, then reduce the heat and simmer gently for 20 minutes, skimming off any scum from time to time. Remove the pan from the heat.

2 Add the lemon rind and sugar to the pan, stir well, and let cool. Strain and add the lemon juice.

3 Taste the lemon barley water and add more sugar, if necessary. Serve chilled with ice and slices of lemon.

QUINOA

Hailed as the supergrain of the future, quinoa (pronounced "keen-wa") is a grain of the past. It was called "the mother grain" by the Incas, who cultivated it for hundreds of years, high in the Andes, solely for their own use.

Nowadays, quinoa is widely available. The tiny, bead-shaped grains have a mild, slightly bitter taste and firm texture. It is cooked in the same way as rice, but the grains quadruple in size, becoming translucent with an unusual white outer ring. Quinoa is useful for making stuffings, pilaffs, bakes, and breakfast cereals.

Health Benefits: Quinoa's supergrain status hails from its rich nutritional value. Unlike other grains, quinoa is a complete protein because it contains all eight essential amino acids. It is an excellent source of calcium, potassium, and zinc as well as iron, magnesium, and B vitamins. It is particularly valuable for people with celiac disease as it is gluten-free.

MILLET

Although millet is usually associated with bird food, it is a highly nutritious grain. It once rivaled barley as the main food of Europe and remains a staple ingredient in many parts of the world, including Africa, China, and India. Its mild flavor makes it an ideal accompaniment to spicy stews and curries, and it can be used as a base for pilaffs or milk puddings. The tiny, firm grains can also be flaked or ground into flour. Millet is gluten-free, so it is a useful food for people with celiac disease. The flour can be used for baking, but needs to be combined with high-gluten flours to make leavened bread.

Health Benefits: Millet is an easily digestible grain. It contains more iron than other grains and is a good source of zinc, calcium, manganese, and B vitamins. It is believed to be beneficial to those suffering from candidiasis, a fungal infection caused by the yeast *Candida albicans*.

Millet

Amaranth

LESSER-KNOWN GRAINS

There are several other grains that deserve a mention, as they are not only becoming more popular, but also are often far richer in nutrients than their better-known counterparts.

Amaranth

This plant, which is native to Mexico, is unusual in that it can be eaten as both a vegetable and a grain. Amaranth is considered a supergrain owing to its excellent nutritional content. The tiny pale seed or "grain" has a strong and distinctive, peppery flavor. It is best used in stews and soups, or it can be ground into flour to make bread, turnovers, and cookies. The flour is gluten-free and has to be mixed with wheat or another flour that contains gluten to make leavened bread. Amaranth leaves are similar to spinach and can be cooked or eaten raw in salads.

Health Benefits: Although its taste may take some getting used to, the nutritional qualities of amaranth more than make up for it. It has more protein than pulses and is rich in amino acids, particularly lysine. Amaranth is also high in iron and calcium.

Kamut

An ancient relative of wheat, this grain has long, slender, brown kernels with a creamy, nutty flavor. It is as versatile as wheat and, when ground into flour, can be used to make pasta, breads, cakes, and pastry. Puffed kamut cereals and kamut crackers are available in health-food stores.

BUCKWHEAT

In spite of its name, buckwheat is not a type of wheat, but is actually related to the rhubarb family. Available plain or toasted, it has a nutty, earthy flavor. It is a staple food in Eastern Europe, as well as Russia, where the triangular grain is milled into a speckled-gray flour and used to make blini. The flour is also used in Japan for soba noodles and in Italy for pasta. Buckwheat pancakes are popular in parts of the United States and France. The whole grain, which is also known as kasha, makes a creamy dessert.

Health Benefits: Like quinoa, buckwheat is a complete protein. It contains all eight essential amino acids, as well as rutin, which aids circulation and helps treat high blood pressure. It is an excellent, sustaining cereal, rich in both iron and some of the B complex vitamins. It is also reputed to be good for the lungs, the kidneys, and the bladder. Buckwheat is gluten-free, and so is useful for people who suffer from celiac disease.

Above, from left: Plain buckwheat, buckwheat flour, and toasted buckwheat

Spelt grain and flour

Health Benefits: Kamut has a higher nutritional value than wheat and is easier to digest. Although it contains gluten, people suffering from celiac disease have found that they can tolerate the grain if eaten in moderation.

Sorghum

This grain is best known for its thick sweet syrup, which is used in cakes and desserts. The grain is similar to millet and is an important, extremely nutritious staple food in Africa and India. It can be used much like rice, and when ground into flour is used to make unleavened bread.

Health Benefits: Sorghum is a useful source of calcium, iron, and B vitamins.

Spelt

This is one of the most ancient cultivated wheats and, because of its high nutritional value, is becoming more widely available. Spelt grain looks very similar to wheat and the flour can be substituted for wheat flour in bread.

Health Benefits: Spelt is richer in vitamins and minerals than wheat, and they are in a more readily digestible form. Although spelt contains gluten, it usually can be tolerated in moderate amounts by people suffering from celiac disease.

Triticale

A hybrid of wheat and rye, triticale was created by Swedish researchers in 1875. It has a sweet, nutty taste and chewy texture, and can be used in the same way as rice, and is ground into flour. It contains more protein than wheat but has less gluten and may need to be mixed with other flours when baking. Triticale flakes can be used in breakfast cereals and crumbles.

Health Benefits: Triticale contains significant amounts of calcium, iron, and B vitamins. It is particularly rich in lysine.

Buying and Storing: To ensure freshness, buy grains in small quantities from a store with a high turnover of stock. Grains can be affected by heat and moisture, and easily become rancid. Store in a dry, cool, dark place.

How to Cook Grains

Grains can be simply boiled in water but, to enhance their flavor, first cook them in a little oil for a few minutes. When they are well coated in oil, add two or three times their volume of water or stock. Bring to a boil, then simmer, covered, until the water is absorbed and the grains are tender. Do not disturb the grains while they are cooking. Other flavorings, such as chopped herbs and whole or ground spices, can be added to the cooking liquid.

Fabulous Fiber

Whole grains are one of the few food groups to contain both soluble and insoluble fiber. The former is prevalent in oats and rye, while wheat, rice, and corn contain insoluble fiber. Both are fundamental to good health and may prevent constipation, ulcers, colitis, colon and rectal cancer, heart disease, diverticulitis, and irritable bowel syndrome. Soluble fiber slows down the absorption of energy from the gut, which means there are no sudden demands on insulin, making it especially important for diabetics.

Kamut

Legumes

Lentils, peas, and pulses provide the cook with a diverse range of flavors and textures. They have long been a staple food in the Middle East, South America, India, and the Mediterranean, but there is hardly a country that does not have its own favorite legume-based dish, from Boston baked beans in the United States to lentil dahl in India. In Mexico, they are spiced and used to make refried beans, while in China they are fermented for black bean and yellow bean sauces. Low in fat and high in complex carbohydrates, vitamins, and minerals, legumes are also an important source of protein for vegetarians and, when eaten with cereals, easily match animal-based sources.

Lentils and Peas

The humble lentil is one of our oldest foods. It originated in Asia and North Africa and continues to be cultivated in those regions, as well as in France and Italy. Lentils are hard even when fresh, so they are always sold dried. Unlike most other pulses, they do not need soaking.

Red lentils

Puy lentils

GREEN AND BROWN LENTILS

Sometimes referred to as continental lentils, these disk-shaped pulses retain their shape when cooked. They take longer to cook than split lentils—about 40–45 minutes—and are ideal for adding to warm salads, casseroles, and stuffings.

Alternatively, green and brown lentils can be cooked and blended with herbs or spices to make a nutritious pâté.

PUY LENTILS

These tiny, dark, blue-green, marbled lentils grow in the Auvergne region in central France. They are considered to be far superior in taste and texture to other varieties, and they retain their bead-like shape during cooking, which takes 25–30 minutes. Puy lentils are a delicious addition to simple dishes such as warm salads, and are also good braised in wine and flavored with fresh herbs.

RED LENTILS

Orange-colored red split lentils, sometimes known as Egyptian lentils, are the most familiar variety. They cook in just 20 minutes, eventually disintegrating into a thick purée. They are ideal for thickening soups and casseroles and, when cooked with spices, make a delicious dahl. In the Middle East, red or yellow lentils are cooked and mixed with spices and vegetables to form balls known as *kofte*.

YELLOW LENTILS

Less well-known, yellow lentils taste very similar to the red variety and are used in much the same way.

PEAS

Dried peas come from the field pea not the garden pea, which is eaten fresh. Unlike lentils, peas are soft when young and require drying. They are available whole or split; the latter have a sweeter flavor and cook more quickly. Like split lentils, split peas do not hold their shape when cooked, making them perfect for dahls, purées, casseroles, and soups.

Green and brown lentils

Cooking Lentils

Lentils are easy to cook and don't need to be soaked. Split red and green lentils cook down to a soft consistency, while whole lentils hold their shape when cooked.

Green, Brown, and Puy Lentils

1 Place generous 1 cup whole lentils in a strainer and rinse under cold running water. Transfer to a saucepan.

2 Cover with water and bring to a boil. Simmer for 25–30 minutes, until tender, replenishing the water if necessary. Drain and season with salt and freshly ground black pepper.

Split Red and Yellow Lentils

1 Place generous 1 cup split lentils in a strainer and rinse under cold running water. Transfer to a saucepan.

2 Cover with 2½ cups water and bring to a boil. Simmer for 20–25 minutes, stirring occasionally, until the water is absorbed and the lentils are tender. Season to taste.

They take about 45 minutes to cook. Marrow fat peas are larger in size and are used to make the traditional British dish "mushy" peas. Like other whole peas, they require soaking overnight before use.

Buying and Storing: Although lentils and peas can be kept for up to a year, they toughen with time. Buy from stores with a fast turnover of stock and store in airtight containers in a cool, dark place. Look for bright, unwrinkled pulses that are not dusty. Rinse well before use.

Health Benefits: Lentils and peas share an impressive range of nutrients including iron, selenium, folate, manganese, zinc, phosphorus, and some B vitamins. Extremely low in fat and richer in protein than most pulses, lentils and peas are reputed to be important in fighting heart disease by reducing harmful LDL cholesterol in the body. They are high in fiber, which aids the functioning of the bowels and colon. Fiber also slows down the rate at which sugar enters the bloodstream, providing a steady supply of energy, which can help control diabetes.

Marrow fat peas (above) and yellow and green split peas

COOK'S TIP

Avoid adding salt to the water when cooking lentils and peas as this prevents them softening. Season when cooked.

Pulses

The edible seeds from plants belonging to the legume family, pulses, which include black-eyed peas and a vast range of beans, are packed with protein, vitamins, minerals, and fiber, and are extremely low in fat. For the cook, their ability to absorb the flavors of other foods means that pulses can be used as the base for an infinite number of dishes. Most pulses require soaking overnight in cold water before use, so it is wise to plan ahead if using the dried type.

Adzuki beans

BLACK BEANS

These shiny, black, kidney-shaped beans are often used in Caribbean cooking. They have a sweetish flavor, and their distinctive color adds a dramatic touch to soups, mixed bean salads, or casseroles.

ADZUKI BEANS

Also known as aduki beans, these tiny, deep-red beans have a sweet, nutty flavor and are popular in Asian dishes. In Chinese cooking, they form the base of red bean paste. Known as the "king of beans" in Japan, the adzuki bean is reputed to be good for the liver and kidneys. They cook quickly and can be used in casseroles and bakes. They are also ground into flour for use in cakes, breads, and pastries.

BLACK-EYED PEAS

Also known as black-eye beans or cow peas, black-eyed peas are an essential ingredient in Creole cooking and some spicy Indian curries. The small, creamy-colored bean is characterized by the black spot on its side where it was once attached to the pod. Good in soups and salads, they can also be added to non-sweet bakes and casseroles, and can be used in place of navy or cannellini beans in a wide variety of dishes.

Black beans (left), black-eyed peas (center), and borlotti beans

---

Cannellini Bean Purée

Cooked cannellini beans make a delicious herb- and garlic-flavored purée. Serve spread on toasted pita bread or to use as a dip with chunky raw vegetable crudités.

INGREDIENTS

2^1/2 cups canned or 1^1/4 cups
    dried cannellini beans
2 tablespoons olive oil
1 large garlic clove, finely chopped
2 shallots, finely chopped
5 tablespoons vegetable stock
2 tablespoons chopped fresh flat
    leaf parsley
1 tablespoon snipped fresh chives
salt and freshly ground black pepper

SERVES 4

1 If using dried beans, soak them overnight in cold water, then drain, and rinse. Place in a saucepan and cover with cold water, then bring to a boil and boil rapidly for 10 minutes. Reduce the heat and simmer for about 1 hour, or until tender. If using canned beans, rinse and drain well.

2 Heat the oil in a saucepan and sauté the garlic and shallots for about 5 minutes, stirring occasionally, until soft. Add the beans, stock, parsley, and seasoning, then cook for a few minutes, until heated through.

3 To make a coarse purée, mash the beans with a potato masher. Alternatively, place in a food processor and process until thick and smooth. Serve sprinkled with snipped chives.

Butter beans

BORLOTTI BEANS

These oval beans have red-streaked, pinkish-brown skin and a bitter-sweet flavor. When cooked, they have a tender, moist texture, which is good in Italian bean and pasta soups, as well as hearty vegetable stews. In most recipes, they are interchangeable with red kidney beans.

FAVA BEANS

These large beans were first cultivated by the ancient Egyptians. Usually eaten in their fresh form, fava beans change in color from green to brown when dried, making them difficult to recognize in their dried state. The outer skin can be very tough and chewy, and some people prefer to remove it after cooking. They can also be bought ready-skinned.

Cannellini beans

Fava beans

LIMA AND BUTTER BEANS

Similar in flavor and appearance, both lima beans and butter beans are characterized by their flattish, kidney shape and soft, mealy texture. Cream-colored butter beans are familiar in Britain and Greece, while lima beans are popular in the United States. In Greek cooking, butter beans are oven-baked with tomato, garlic, and olive oil until tender and creamy. The pale-green lima bean is the main ingredient in succotash, a traditional dish that also includes corn kernels. Lima and butter beans are also good with creamy herb sauces. Care should be taken not to overcook both lima and butter beans as they become pulpy and mushy in texture.

CANNELLINI BEANS

These small, white, kidney-shaped beans have a soft, creamy texture when cooked and are popular in Italian cooking. They can be used in place of navy beans and, when dressed with olive oil, lemon juice, crushed garlic, and chopped fresh parsley, make an excellent warm salad.

GARBANZO BEANS

Also known as chick-peas, robust and hearty garbanzo beans resemble shelled hazelnuts and have a delicious nutty flavor and creamy texture. They need lengthy cooking and are much used in Mediterranean and Middle Eastern cooking. In India, they are known as gram and are ground into flour to make fritters and flat breads. Gram flour, also called besan, can be found in health-food stores and Asian grocery stores.

FLAGEOLET BEANS

These young navy beans are removed from the pod before they are fully ripe, hence their fresh delicate flavor. A pretty, mint-green color, they are the most expensive bean to buy and are best treated simply. Cook them until they are tender, then season, and drizzle with a little olive oil and lemon juice.

NAVY BEANS

Most commonly used for canned baked beans, these versatile, ivory-colored beans are small and oval in shape. Also called haricot or Boston beans, they suit slow-cooked dishes, such as casseroles and bakes.

Garbanzo beans

PINTO BEANS

A smaller, paler version of the borlotti bean, the savoury-tasting pinto has an attractive speckled skin—it is aptly called the painted bean. One of the many relatives of the kidney bean, pinto beans feature extensively in Mexican cooking,

most familiarly in refried beans, when they are cooked until tender and fried with garlic, chile, and tomatoes. The beans are then mashed, resulting in a wonderful, spicy, rough purée that is usually served with warm tortillas. Sour cream and garlic-flavored guacamole are good accompaniments.

RED KIDNEY BEANS

Glossy, mahogany-red kidney beans retain their color and shape when cooked. They have a soft, mealy texture and are much used in South American cooking. An essential ingredient in spicy chiles, they can also be used to make refried beans (although this dish is traditionally made from pinto beans). Cooked kidney beans can be used to make a variety of salads, but they are especially good combined with red onion and chopped flat leaf parsley and mint, then tossed in an olive oil dressing.

It is essential to follow the cooking instructions when preparing kidney beans, as they contain a substance that causes severe poisoning if they are not boiled vigorously for 10–15 minutes.

Above, clockwise from left: Navy beans, red kidney beans, flageolet beans and pinto beans

Cooking Kidney Beans

Most types of beans, with the exception of adzuki beans and mung beans, require soaking for 5–6 hours or overnight and then boiling rapidly for 10–15 minutes to remove any harmful toxins. This is particularly important for kidney beans, which can cause serious poisoning if not treated in this way.

1 Wash the beans well, then place in a bowl that allows plenty of room for expansion. Cover with cold water and let soak overnight or for 8–12 hours, then drain and rinse.

2 Place the beans in a large saucepan and cover with fresh cold water. Bring to a boil and boil rapidly for 10–15 minutes, then reduce the heat and simmer for 1–1½ hours until tender. Drain and serve.

The Flatulence-free Bean
The American space program NASA is involved in research into flatulence-free foods. One such food is the manteca bean, discovered by Dr Colin Leakey in Chile. This small, yellow bean is flatulence-free and easy to digest. It is now being grown both in Cambridgeshire, England and the Channel Islands, and should become more widely available, called either manteca beans or Jersey yellow beans.

FUL MEDAMES

A member of the fava bean family, these small Egyptian beans form the base of the national dish of the same name, in which they are flavored with ground cumin and then baked with olive oil, garlic, and lemon, and

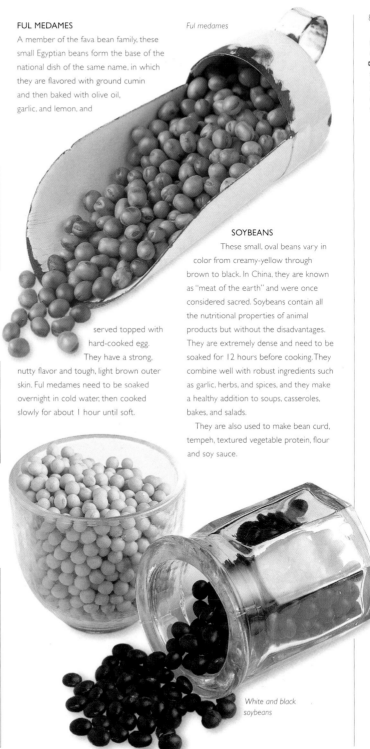

Ful medames

served topped with hard-cooked egg. They have a strong, nutty flavor and tough, light brown outer skin. Ful medames need to be soaked overnight in cold water, then cooked slowly for about 1 hour until soft.

SOYBEANS

These small, oval beans vary in color from creamy-yellow through brown to black. In China, they are known as "meat of the earth" and were once considered sacred. Soybeans contain all the nutritional properties of animal products but without the disadvantages. They are extremely dense and need to be soaked for 12 hours before cooking. They combine well with robust ingredients such as garlic, herbs, and spices, and they make a healthy addition to soups, casseroles, bakes, and salads.

They are also used to make bean curd, tempeh, textured vegetable protein, flour and soy sauce.

White and black soybeans

How to Prepare and Cook Pulses

There is much debate as to whether soaking pulses before cooking is necessary, but it certainly reduces cooking times, and can enhance flavor by starting the germination process. First, wash pulses under cold running water, then place in a bowl of fresh cold water, and let soak overnight. Discard any pulses that float to the surface, drain, and rinse again. Put in a large saucepan and cover with fresh cold water. Boil rapidly for 10–15 minutes, then reduce the heat, cover, and simmer until tender.

Cooking Times for Pulses

As cooking times can vary depending on the age of the pulses, this table should be used as a general guide.

Adzuki beans	30–45 minutes
Black beans	1 hour
Black-eyed peas	1–1¼ hours
Borlotti beans	1–1½ hours
Cannellini beans	1 hour
Fava beans	1½ hours
Flageolet beans	1½ hours
Ful medames	1 hour
Garbanzo beans	1½–2½ hours
Kidney beans	1–1½ hours
Lima/butter beans	1–1¼ hours
Mung beans	25–40 minutes
Navy beans	1–1½ hours
Pinto beans	1–1¼ hours
Soybeans	2 hours

MUNG BEANS

Instantly recognizable in their sprouted form as bean sprouts, mung or moong beans are small, olive-colored beans native to India. They are soft and sweet when cooked, and are used in the spicy curry, moong dahl. Soaking is not essential, but if they are soaked overnight, this will reduce the usual 40 minutes cooking time by about half.

Mung beans

Using Canned Beans

Canned beans are convenient storecupboard stand-bys, because they require no soaking or lengthy cooking. Choose canned beans that do not have added sugar or salt, and rinse well and drain before use. The canning process reduces the levels of vitamins and minerals, but canned beans still contain reputable amounts.

Canned beans tend to be softer than cooked, dried beans so they are easy to mash, which makes them good for pâtés, stuffings, croquettes, and rissoles, but they can also be used to make quick salads. They can, in fact, be used for any dish that calls for cooked, dried beans: a drained 15-ounce can is roughly the equivalent of ¾ cup dried beans. Firmer canned beans, such as kidney beans, can be added to stews and re-cooked, but softer beans, such as navy beans, should be just heated through.

Buying and Storing: Look for plump, shiny beans with unbroken skin. Beans toughen with age so, although they will keep for up to a year in a cool, dry place, it is best to buy them in small quantities from stores with a regular turnover of stock. Avoid beans that look dusty or dirty and store them in an airtight container in a cool, dark, dry place.

Health Benefits: The health attributes of beans are plentiful. They are packed with protein, soluble and insoluble fiber, iron, potassium, phosphorous, manganese, magnesium, folate, and most B vitamins.

Soybeans are the most nutritious of all beans. Rich in high-quality protein, this wonder-pulse contains all eight essential amino acids that cannot be synthesized by the body but are vital for the renewal of cells and tissues.

Insoluble fiber ensures regular bowel movements, while soluble fiber has been found to lower blood cholesterol, thereby reducing the risk of heart disease and stroke. Studies show that eating dried beans on a regular basis can lower cholesterol levels by almost 20 percent. Beans contain a concentration of lignins, also known as phytoestrogens, which protect against cancer of the breast, prostate, and colon. Lignins may also help to balance hormone levels in the body.

COOK'S TIPS

• If you are short of time, the long soaking process can be speeded up: first, cook the beans in boiling water for 2 minutes, then remove the pan from the heat. Cover and leave for about 2 hours. Drain, rinse, and cover with plenty of fresh cold water before cooking.

• Cooking beans in a pressure cooker will reduce the cooking time by around three-quarters.

• Do not add salt to beans while they are cooking as this will cause them to toughen. Cook the beans first, then season with salt and pepper. Acid foods, such as tomatoes, lemons, or vinegar will also toughen beans, so only add these ingredients once the beans are soft.

Quick Cooking and Serving Ideas for Pulses

• To flavor beans, add an onion, garlic, herbs, or spices before cooking. Remove whole flavorings before serving.

• Spoon spicy, red lentil dahl and some crisp, fried onions on top of a warm tortilla, then roll up, and eat.

• Dress cooked beans with extra virgin olive oil, lemon juice, crushed garlic, diced tomato, and fresh basil.

• Mix cooked garbanzo beans, scallions, olives, and chopped parsley, then drizzle with olive oil and lemon juice.

• Mash cooked beans with olive oil, garlic, and cilantro and pile onto toasted bread. Top with a poached egg.

• Fry cooked red kidney beans in olive oil with chopped onion, chile, garlic, and fresh cilantro leaves.

• Sauté a little chopped garlic in olive oil, add cooked or canned flageolet beans, canned tomatoes, and chopped fresh chile, then cook for a few minutes, until the sauce has thickened slightly and the beans are heated through.

• Roast cooked garbanzo beans, which have been drizzled with olive oil and garlic, for 20 minutes at 400°F, then toss in a little ground cumin and sprinkle with chile flakes. Serve with chunks of feta cheese and nan bread.

Soybean Products

Soybeans are incredibly versatile and are used to make an extensive array of by-products that are used in cooking— tofu, tempeh, textured vegetable protein, flour, miso, and a variety of sauces. The soybean is the most nutritious of all beans. Rich in high-quality protein, it is one of the few vegetarian foods that contains all eight essential amino acids that cannot be synthesized in the body and are vital for the renewal of cells and tissues.

TOFU

Also known as bean curd, tofu is made in a similar way to soft cheese. The beans are boiled, mashed, and strained to make soy "milk," and the "milk" is then curdled using a coagulant. The resulting curds are drained and pressed to make tofu, and there are several different types to choose from.

Firm tofu

This type of bean curd is sold in blocks and can be cubed or sliced, and used in vegetable stir-fries, kebabs, salads, soups, and casseroles. Alternatively, firm tofu can be mashed and used in bakes and burgers. The bland flavor of firm tofu is improved by marinating, because its porous texture readily absorbs flavors and seasonings.

Silken tofu

Soft with a silky, smooth texture, this type of bean curd is ideal for use in sauces, dressings, dips, and soups. It is a useful dairy-free alternative to cream, soft cheese, or yogurt, and can be used to make creamy desserts.

Other forms of tofu

Smoked, marinated, and deep-fried tofu are all readily available in health-food stores and Asian stores, as well as in some supermarkets.

Deep-fried tofu is fairly tasteless, but it has an interesting texture. It puffs up during cooking, and under the golden, crisp coating the tofu is white and soft, and easily absorbs the flavor of other ingredients. It can be used in the same way as firm tofu and, as it has been fried in vegetable oil, it is suitable for vegetarians.

Buying and Storing: All types of fresh bean curd can be kept in the fridge for up to 1 week. Firm tofu should be kept covered in water, which must be changed regularly. Freezing tofu is not recommended because it alters the texture. Silken tofu is often available in long-life vacuum packs, which do not have to be kept in the fridge and have a much longer shelf-life.

TEMPEH

This Indonesian specialty is made by fermenting cooked soybeans with a cultured starter. Tempeh is similar to tofu, but has a nuttier, more savory flavor. It can be used in the same way as firm tofu and also benefits from marinating. While some types of bean curd are regarded as a dairy replacement, the firmer texture of tempeh means that it can be used instead of meat in pies and casserole dishes.

Buying and Storing: Tempeh is available chilled or frozen in health-food stores and Asian stores. Chilled tempeh can be stored in the fridge for up to a week. Frozen tempeh can be left in the freezer for 1 month; thaw before use.

BEAN CURD SKINS AND STICKS

Made from soy "milk," dried bean curd skins and sticks, like fresh bean curd, have neither aroma nor flavor until they are cooked, when they will rapidly absorb the flavor of seasonings and other ingredients. They are used in Chinese cooking and

Above, clockwise from left: Silken tofu, bean curd skins, firm tofu, and marinated tofu

TVP

Textured vegetable protein, or TVP, is a useful meat replacement and is usually bought in dry chunks or ground. Made from processed soybeans, TVP is very versatile and readily absorbs the strong flavors of ingredients such as herbs, spices, and vegetable stock. It is inexpensive and is a convenient storecupboard item. TVP needs to be rehydrated in boiling water or vegetable stock, and can be used in stews and curries, or as a filling for pies.

Tempeh

need to be soaked until pliable before use. Bean curd skins should be soaked for an hour or two and can be used to wrap a variety of fillings.

Bean curd sticks need to be soaked for several hours or overnight. They can be chopped and added to soups, stir-fries, and casseroles.

Tofu Fruit Fool

1 Place a packet of silken tofu in the bowl of a food processor. Add some soft fruit or berries—for example, strawberries, raspberries, or blackberries.

2 Process the mixture to form a smooth purée, then sweeten to taste with a little honey, maple syrup, or corn malt syrup.

Marinated Tofu Kebabs

Tofu is relatively tasteless, but readily takes on other flavors. It is at its best when marinated in aromatic oils, soy sauce, spices, and herbs.

1 Cut a block of tofu into ½-inch cubes and marinate in a mixture of peanut oil, sesame oil, soy sauce, crushed garlic, grated fresh ginger root, and honey for at least 1 hour.

2 Thread the cubes of tofu onto skewers with chunks of zucchini, onions, and mushrooms. Brush with the marinade and broil or grill until golden, turning occasionally.

Legumes

Soy flour

SOY FLOUR

This is a finely ground, high-protein flour, which is also gluten-free. It is often mixed with other flours in bread and pastries, adding a pleasant nuttiness, or it can be used as a thickener in sauces.

Buying and Storing: Store TVP and soy flour in an airtight container in a cool, dry, dark place.

SOY SAUCE

This soy by-product originated over 2,000 years ago and the recipe has changed little since then. It is made by combining crushed soybeans with wheat, salt, water, and a yeast-based culture called *koji*, and the mixture is left to ferment for between 6 months and 3 years.

There are two basic types of soy sauce: light and dark. Light soy sauce is slightly thinner in consistency and saltier. It is used in dressings and soups. Dark soy sauce is heavier and sweeter, with a more rounded flavor, and is used in marinades, stir-fries, and sauces. Try to buy naturally brewed soy sauce as many other kinds are now chemically prepared to hasten the fermentation process, and may contain flavorings and colorings.

SHOYU

Made in Japan, shoyu is aged for 1–2 years to produce a full-flavored sauce that can be used in the same way as dark soy sauce. You can buy it in health-food stores and Asian foodstores.

TAMARI

This form of soy sauce is a natural by-product of making miso, although it is often produced in the same way as soy sauce. Most tamari is made without wheat, which means that it is gluten-free. It has a rich, dark, robust flavor and is used in cooking or as a condiment.

Buying and Storing: Keep soy sauce, shoyu, and tamari in a cool, dark place.

MISO

This thick paste is made from a mixture of cooked soybeans, rice, wheat or barley, salt, and water, and is left to ferment for up to 3 years. Miso can be used to add a savory flavor to soups, stocks, stir-fries, and noodle dishes, and is a staple food in Asia. There are three main types: kome, or white miso, which is the lightest and sweetest; medium-strength mugi miso, which has a mellow flavor and is preferred for everyday use; and hacho miso, which is a dark chocolate color, and has a thick texture and a strong flavor.

Soybean Sauces

Black bean sauce Made from fermented black soybeans, this has a rich, thick consistency and a salty, full flavor. It should always be heated before use to bring out the flavor. Fermented black beans, which Chinese cooks use to make homemade black bean sauce, can be bought in vacuum-packs or cans from Asian stores.

Yellow bean sauce Produced from fermented yellow soybeans, this sauce has an intense flavor.

Hoisin sauce A thick red-brown sauce made from soybeans, flour, garlic, chile, sesame oil, and vinegar. Mainly intended as a marinade, it can be used as a dipping sauce.

Kecap manis An Indonesian-style dark, sweet soy sauce, which can be found in Asian stores.

Ground and cubed textured vegetable protein (TVP)

Buying and Storing: Miso keeps well and can be stored for several months, but should be kept in the fridge once it has been opened.

Health Benefits: Soy is one of today's healthiest foods. Rich in minerals, particularly iron and calcium, it is also low in saturated fats and is cholesterol-free. It has the ability to help reduce osteoporosis, blood pressure, and blood cholesterol, and there is evidence to suggest that it can help reduce the risk of cancer.

Japanese women (whose diets are rich in soy) have a lower incidence of breast cancer than women who consume a typical Western diet. Likewise, Japanese men have a lower incidence of prostate cancer than Western men. This is thought to be because soy contains hormone-like substances called phytoestrogens.

Studies have also shown that eating miso on a regular basis can increase the body's natural resistance to radiation. Additionally, miso is said to prevent cancer of the liver, and it can also help to expel toxins from the body.

Light soy sauce (below) and dark soy sauce

Watch Point

Although soybeans and products are nutritionally beneficial, they are also common allergens and can provoke reactions such as headaches and digestive problems. Avoid eating excessive amounts of soy, and always cook sprouted soybeans before use.

Mugi miso (left) and hacha miso

Tamari (left) and shoyu

Dairy Foods and Alternatives

Some people may question the inclusion of dairy products in a whole food cookbook, and while it would be foolish to advocate the consumption of vast quantities of high-fat milk, cream, and cheese, a diet that includes moderate amounts of dairy products does provide valuable vitamins and minerals. There is little reason to reject dairy products as they can enrich vegetarian cooking. However, for those who choose to avoid dairy foods, there are plenty of alternatives.

Milk, Cream, and Yogurt

This wide group of ingredients includes milk, cream, and yogurt made from cow, goat, and sheep milk, as well as non-dairy products, such as soy "milk" and "cream" and other non-dairy "milks," which are made from nuts and grains. They are used in a huge range of sweet and non-sweet dishes, from sauces and soups to drinks and desserts.

MILK

Often referred to as a complete food, milk is one of our most widely used ingredients. Cow's milk remains the most popular type although, with the growing concern about saturated fat and cholesterol, low-fat and skim milks now outsell the full-fat version. Skim milk contains half the calories of full-fat milk and only a fraction of the fat, but nutritionally it is on a par, retaining its vitamins, calcium, and other minerals.

Buy organic milk if you can, because it comes from cows that have been fed on a pesticide-free diet, and are not routinely treated with hormones, antibiotics, or BST (bovine somatotrophin), which is used in some countries to boost the milk yield from cows.

Sour cream and crème fraîche

Goat and sheep milk

These milks make useful alternatives for people who are intolerant to cow milk. The lactose in cow milk can cause severe indigestion, and an intolerance to dairy products often manifests itself in eczema or sinus congestion. Goat and sheep milk are nutritionally similar to cow milk, but are easier to digest.

Goat milk has a distinctive, musky flavor, while sheep milk is a little creamier and has a less assuming flavor.

CREAM

The high fat content of cream means that it is not an ingredient to be eaten lavishly on a daily basis. Used with discretion, however, cream lends a richness to soups, sauces, bakes, and desserts.

The fat content of cream ranges enormously: half-cream contains about 12 percent, light cream 18 percent, heavy 48 percent, and clotted cream, which is the highest, contains about 55 percent.

From left: Goat, cow, and sheep milk, and soy "milk"

Smetana

SOUR CREAM

This thick-textured cream is treated with lactic acid, which gives it its characteristic tang. Full-fat sour cream contains about 20 percent fat, although low- and non-fat versions are available. It can be used in the same way as cream. Care should be taken when cooking, as it can curdle if heated to too high a temperature.

CREME FRAICHE

This rich, cultured cream is similar to sour cream, but its high fat content, at around 35 percent, means that it does not curdle when cooked. Crème fraîche is delicious served with fresh fruit, such as ripe summer berries, puréed mangoes, or sliced bananas.

BUTTERMILK

Traditionally made from the milky liquid left over after butter making, buttermilk is now more likely to be made from skim milk, mixed with milk solids and then cultured with lactic acid. It has a creamy, mild, sour taste and makes a tangy and distinctive addition to desserts. Used in baking, buttermilk gives cakes and soda bread a moist texture. It is low in fat, containing only 0.1 percent.

SMETANA

Originally made in Russia, this rich version of buttermilk is made from skim milk and single cream with an added culture. It has a similar fat content to strained yogurt (about 10 percent), and should be treated in the same way. Smetana can curdle if it is overheated.

Buying and Storing: When buying milk, cream, and cream-related products, don't forget to check the label. Manufacturers and retailers are obliged to give a "best before" or "sell-by" date on the packet. The fat content, nutritional information, and list of ingredients will also be

Buttermilk

detailed. Try to avoid products that contain unnecessary additives or flavorings. For instance, low-fat crème fraîche, yogurts, and cream may contain animal-based gelatin, which acts as a thickener. Store dairy products in the fridge and consume within a few days of opening. Long-life cartons will keep indefinitely but once opened, must be treated as fresh and kept in the fridge.

Health Benefits: Milk is an important source of calcium and phosphorus, both of which are essential for healthy teeth and bones, and are said to prevent osteoporosis. Milk also contains significant amounts of zinc and the B vitamins, including B_{12}, along with a small amount of vitamin D. Numerous studies have revealed that, due to its high calcium content, milk fortified with vitamin D may have a role in preventing colon cancer. The antibodies found in milk may boost the immune system and help gastrointestinal problems, and skim milk may reduce the amount of cholesterol produced by the liver.

Above, clockwise from bottom left: Whipping cream, light cream, and whipped heavy cream

Dairy Foods and Alternatives

Apart from soy "milk", non-dairy "milks" or drinks are usually either nut- or grain-based. They can be used as a substitute for regular milk in a wide variety of sweet and non-sweet dishes, such as milk puddings, custards, hot and cold milk drinks, and sauces, but shouldn't be overheated or cooked for too long or they may curdle.

Oat "milk" Made from oat kernels and either vegetable or sunflower oil, this nutritious drink is high in fiber.

Rice "milk" With a similar consistency to soy "milk", rice "milk" is also non-mucous forming. Rice "milk" is easily digested and almost non-allergenic.

Nut "milk" Crushed and ground almonds or cashew nuts are mixed with water to form this mild-tasting non-dairy "milk".

Clockwise from left: "Milks" made from rice, almonds, and oats

Making Yogurt

It is easy to make yogurt at home—simply make sure that you use live yogurt as a starter and that it is as fresh as possible. Once you have made the first batch, you can reserve some of the yogurt as a starter for the next. Don't use too much starter or the yogurt may become sour and grainy. Yogurt can be flavored with fresh or dried fruit, or honey, or to make a more substantial dish, stir in soaked oats, chopped nuts, and toasted seeds.

1 Pour 2½ cups whole, low-fat, or skim milk into a saucepan and bring to a boil. Remove the pan from the heat and let the milk cool to 113°F.

2 If you don't have a thermometer, you can use your finger—the milk should feel slightly hotter than is comfortable. Pour the warm milk into a medium-size, sterilized bowl.

3 Whisk in 1–2 tablespoons live yogurt—this acts as a starter. Leave in the bowl or transfer it to a large jar.

4 Cover the bowl or jar with plastic wrap, then insulate the bowl or jar with several layers of dish cloths, and place in a warm airing cupboard. Alternatively, the yogurt can be transferred to a vacuum flask to keep it warm. Leave for 10–12 hours until set. Transfer to the fridge.

SOY SUBSTITUTES

Soy "milk"

This is the most widely used alternative to milk. Made from pulverized soybeans, it is suitable for both cooking and drinking and is used to make yogurt, cream, and cheese. Soy "milk" is interchangeable with cow milk, although it has a slightly thicker consistency and a nutty flavor. Fruit- and chocolate-flavored soy "milk", and versions fortified with extra vitamins, are widely available in heath food stores and larger supermarkets.

Soy "cream"

This is made from a higher proportion of beans than that in soy "milk", which gives it a richer flavor and thicker texture. It has a similar consistency to light cream and can be used in the same ways.

Buying and Storing: Most soy "milks" and "creams" are sold in long-life cartons, which extends their shelf-life and means that they do not require refrigeration until opened. Buy soy "milk" that is fortified with extra vitamins and calcium and, depending on how you intend to use it, choose the sweetened or unsweetened variety. Some retailers stock fresh soy "milk" and this should be treated in the same way as cow milk.

Health Benefits: Soy "milk" and "cream" are a valuable source of protein, calcium, iron, magnesium, phosphorus, and vitamin E. The "milk" is low in calories and contains no cholesterol. Numerous studies have shown that soy can reduce the risk of certain cancers, heart disease, kidney disease, and osteoporosis.

YOGURT

Praised for its health-giving qualities, yogurt has earned a reputation as one of the most valuable health foods. The fat content ranges from 0.5 grams per 100 grams for very low-fat or virtually fat-free yogurts to 4 grams per 100 grams for wholemilk yogurt. The consistency may be thin or thick. Greek-style yogurt, which is made from cow or sheep milk, contains about 10 grams of fat per 100 grams— just enough to prevent it from curdling during cooking. However, although it is higher in fat than other types of yogurt, it contains less fat than cream and makes a healthier alternative. Lower-fat yogurts can also be used instead of cream, but are best used in uncooked dishes. Strained yogurt has its watery whey removed to

make it thicker and richer, and has a similar fat content to Greek-style yogurts. When buying yogurt, look for "live" on the label. This signifies that it has been fermented with a starter culture bacteria (usually *Lactobacillus bulgaricus* or *Streptococcus thermophilous*), which is beneficial to health. Bio yogurts, which contain extra bacteria (often *Lactobacillus acidophilus* or *Bifidobacterium bifidum*), have a milder flavor than other yogurts, and may have wider healing benefits.

Buying and Storing: Yogurt has a limited shelf-life, so it is important to check the "best before" or "sell-by" date on the label. Although yogurt making is essentially a natural process, many manufacturers add unnecessary amounts of sugar, colorings, flavorings, and other additives, such as thickeners and stabilizers. Some yogurts, especially low-fat varieties, may contain gelatin, an animal by-product. Low-calorie yogurts usually contain artificial sweeteners. Fruit yogurts may contain a high amount of sugar, as well as colorings and flavorings; check the label before buying, and choose varieties that have a high fruit content—those with the highest amount will mention fruit first in the list of ingredients. More expensive, specialty yogurts may be the least adulterated.

Health Benefits: Yogurt is rich in calcium, phosphorus, and B vitamins. The bacteria present in live yogurt ensure that it is easily digestible: it may stimulate the friendly bacteria in the gut and suppress harmful bacteria, so aiding digestion and relieving gastrointestinal problems. Evidence suggests that yogurt can help protect against vaginal thrush and may be applied externally.

Live and bio yogurts have extra health benefits, although their levels of good bacteria can vary. The bacteria in bio yogurt may help boost natural resistance to food poisoning and tummy bugs and, if eaten after a course of antibiotics, may restore the internal flora of the intestines. There is also evidence to suggest that bio yogurt that contains the *acidophilus* culture could prevent cancer of the colon.

Cooking with Yogurt

Yogurt is a useful culinary ingredient, but does not respond well to heating. It is best added at the end of cooking, just before serving, to prevent it from curdling and to retain its vital bacteria. High-fat yogurts are more stable, but it is possible to stabilize and thicken low-fat yogurt by stirring in a little blended cornstarch before cooking. Unsweetened yogurt can be used in a wide range of sweet and non-sweet dishes, and it makes a calming addition to hot curries.

Clockwise from top left: Thick cow milk yogurt, thin cow milk yogurt, Greek-style yogurt, soy yogurt, goat milk yogurt, and sheep milk yogurt

Soft and Hard Cheeses

The selection of cheeses in this section is a mere fraction of the extensive range that is available in good cheese stores and supermarkets. Some, like mozzarella and feta, are more often cooked in pies or on pizzas, or used in salads, while others, like the soft, white, Camembert-type goat cheeses, make a good addition to a cheese board.

MOZZARELLA

This delicate, silky-white cheese is usually made from cow milk, although authentically it should be made from buffalo milk. The sweet milky balls of cheese have excellent melting qualities, hence its use on pizzas and in bakes, but it is equally delicious served in salads. When combined with avocado and tomato it makes the classic Italian three-color salad.

FETA

Believed to be one of the first cheeses, feta is curdled naturally without the addition of rennet. Although it was once made with goat or sheep milk, it is now more often made with milk from cows. It is preserved in brine, hence its saltiness, and has a firm, crumbly texture. It is used in the classic Greek salad with cucumber, tomatoes, and olives. To reduce the salty taste of feta, rinse it in water, then let soak in cold water for 10 minutes.

Feta, which is packed in brine, can be bought as small rounds or larger blocks

GOAT CHEESE

Indispensable for those intolerant or allergic to cow milk, goat cheese varieties range from soft, mild and creamy through a Camembert-type, which has a soft center and downy rind, to the firm Cheddar alternative. Similarly, the flavor of goat cheese spans from fresh, creamy and mild to sharp and pungent.

HALLOUMI

This ancient cheese was first made by nomadic Bedouin tribes. It is commonly sold in small blocks, and is often sprinkled with mint. Halloumi has a firm, rubbery texture and retains its shape when broiled or fried. Some people consider it to be the vegetarian alternative to bacon.

CHEDDAR

Unfortunately, much of the Cheddar sold today is made in factories. Avoid these fairly tasteless, rubbery blocks and look for traditional farmhouse Cheddar, which is matured for between nine and 24 months, and has a rich, strong, savory flavor.

Mozzarella

Goat cheese comes in a multitude of different forms

Halloumi

Health Benefits: Semisoft cheeses, such as mozzarella, and hard cheeses, such as Parmesan and Cheddar, contain valuable amounts of calcium, protein, vitamins, and minerals. Hard cheeses are also high in saturated fat. When buying hard cheeses, choose a sharp, good-quality type, as the strong flavor means that relatively small quantities are needed to add flavor to a dish. Saturated fat is known to increase blood cholesterol, which can lead to heart disease and stroke, so always eat cheese in moderation. On the plus side, research shows that cheese—particularly a waxy, hard cheese like Cheddar—eaten after a meal, may reduce the likelihood of tooth decay by as much as 50 percent.

Non-dairy Cheeses

Soy cheese is the most common non-dairy variety. It can lack the depth of flavor of cheese made from cow, goat, or sheep milk, but it is nevertheless a valuable alternative for people who prefer not to buy dairy products or who are lactose intolerant. Soy cheese is made from a blend of processed soybeans and vegetable fats and may be flavored with herbs and spices. Other non-dairy cheeses include a Parmesan-type cheese made from rice and a spice-flavored cheese produced from nuts.

PARMESAN

Allowed to mature for at least 18 months and up to four years, this richly flavored cheese may be high in fat—although not as high as Cheddar—but a little goes a long way. Avoid ready-grated Parmesan and opt for a chunk freshly cut off the block. Parmesan keeps for a long time in the fridge and is excellent grated and added to pasta, risottos, and bakes, or shaved over salads.

Buying and Storing: Hard cheeses are best stored in a cool pantry but, if kept in the fridge, the cheese should be left at room temperature for at least an hour before eating. Cheese starts to dry out as soon as it is cut, so keep it loosely wrapped in foil or waxed paper.

Parmesan

Fresh Unripened Cheeses

As their name suggests, fresh unripened cheeses are young and immature. They have a light, mild taste that readily accepts stronger flavored ingredients, such as herbs and spices. Their high moisture content means that they are lower in fat and are less likely to induce migraines. Fresh cheeses can be used in both non-sweet dishes and desserts.

FROMAGE FRAIS

This smooth, fresh cheese has the same consistency as thick yogurt, but is less acidic. It can be used in the same way as yogurt: mixed with fruit purée to make fools; combined with dried fruit, nuts, and grains; or in sweet and non-sweet tarts. The fat content varies from almost nothing to about 8 percent. Full-fat fromage frais is the best choice for cooking, as it is less likely to separate.

RICOTTA

A soft, low-fat unsalted cheese, which can be made from sheep, goat, or cow milk, ricotta has a slightly granular texture and is widely used in Italian cooking. Its mild, clean flavor means that it is incredibly versatile. It makes a neutral base for crêpe fillings, and can be used as a stuffing for pasta, when it is often combined with spinach. Ricotta is also good in tarts, cakes, and cheesecakes, or it can be served simply on its own with fruit. Mixed with herbs and garlic, it make a tasty sandwich filling.

Below, clockwise from left: Ricotta, fromage frais, quark, cream cheese, and cottage cheese

QUARK

This low-fat cheese is usually made with low-fat or skim milk. Its mild, slightly tangy flavor and light, creamy texture make it perfect in cheesecakes and desserts, or it can be diluted with milk to make an alternative to cream. In northern European countries, it is used as a spread instead of butter.

COTTAGE CHEESE

Lower in fat than most other cheeses (between 2 and 5 percent), cottage cheese is not usually used for cooking, but is good in salads and dips. It makes a fine accompaniment to soft fruits and is best eaten as fresh as possible.

CREAM CHEESE

Commonly used in cheesecakes, dips, and spreads, this cheese has a rich, velvety consistency, mild flavor, and a high fat content—about 35 percent—although it is possible to buy lower-fat alternatives made from skim milk.

NON-DAIRY SOFT CHEESES

A wide range of soft, soy-based cheeses is available from health-food stores. They are a valuable alternative for people who prefer not to buy dairy products.

Buying and Storing: Fresh unripened cheeses do not keep for very long and are best bought in small quantities and eaten soon after purchase. Store in an airtight container in the fridge.

Health Benefits: Fresh unripened cheeses generally have a lower fat content than hard cheeses and are less likely to trigger migraines. They also provide plenty of protein, calcium, and vitamin B_{12}.

> **Always Read the Label**
>
> Check the labels on low-fat yogurts and soft cheeses as these products sometimes contain animal-derived gelatin, which is used as a setting agent. Until relatively recently, the rennet use for cheese-making was obtained from animals. Nowadays, however, vegetarian rennet is more widely used, although this may not be mentioned on the pack. If in doubt, check with the manufacturer.

Making Fresh Soft Cheese

Fresh soft cheese can be made using sour milk (made from milk mixed with yogurt) or sour cream. Use unsweetened or sweeten with honey, orange flower water, or soft fruit. Alternatively, mix with chopped fresh herbs and garlic.

1 Place 4 cups low-fat milk and ½ cup live yogurt or sour cream in a heavy-based saucepan and mix thoroughly. Bring to a boil, lower the heat, then simmer for 5 minutes, or until the milk curdles, stirring continuously.

2 Line a metal strainer or colander with cheesecloth and place over a large bowl. Pour the milk mixture into it and let drain for 1 hour, or until it stops dripping. Alternatively, gather together the edges of the cheesecloth, tie with string, and suspend over the bowl for about 1 hour, until it stops dripping.

3 The residue in the cheesecloth is the soft cheese. Store in a covered bowl in the fridge for 3–4 days.

Butter Versus Margarine

Whether butter is better than margarine has been the focus of much debate. The taste, especially of good-quality, farmhouse butter, is certainly superior to margarine. However, butter, which contains 80 percent saturated fat, has the ability to raise cholesterol levels in the body.

Vegetable margarine contains the same amount of fat as butter, but the fat is polyunsaturated, which was once considered to give margarine greater health benefits. Unfortunately, margarine manufacturing processes change the fats into trans fats, or hydrogenated fats. Studies have shown that trans fats may be more likely than the saturated fat in butter to damage the heart and blood vessels. In addition, cooking removes many of the health benefits of polyunsaturated fats.

SPREADS

Lower-fat margarines are known as spreads. They contain less than 80 percent fat and those that are under 65 percent fat can be classified as reduced-fat. When the fat content falls below 41 percent, a spread can be called low-fat or half-fat. Very low-fat spreads may contain gelatin, and their high water content means they are not suitable for cooking. Olive-oil based spreads are rich in monounsaturated fats and are said to reduce cholesterol levels. They can be used for cooking.

Buying and Storing: When buying margarine and spreads always choose good-quality brands that contain no hydrogenated fats. Butter, margarines, and spreads absorb other flavors, so they need to be kept well-wrapped. Always store these products in the fridge; unsalted butters will keep for up to 2 weeks, other butters for up to a month, and margarines and spreads will keep for about 2 months.

Below: There is a wide variety of different butters, margarines, and spreads available. Whichever you choose to use, don't consume too much of these high-fat foods.

Eggs

An inexpensive, self-contained source of nourishment, hen eggs offer the cook tremendous scope, whether served simply solo or as part of a dish. There are several different types, but the best are organic, free-range eggs from a small producer.

ORGANIC FREE-RANGE EGGS

These eggs are from hens that are fed on a natural pesticide-free diet, which has not had hormones or artificial colorants added. The hens are able to roam on land that has not been treated with chemical fertilizers and is certified organic. Free-range hens have the same indoor conditions as barn hens, but also have daytime access to the open air.

It is important to note that eggs can be either free-range or organic, without being both. Check the labeling carefully, or ask the seller to confirm the details.

Organic free-range eggs

SIZE

Several factors influence the size of an egg. The major factor is the size of the hen. As the hen ages, her eggs increase in size. Egg sizes are Jumbo, Extra Large, Medium, Small and Peewee. Medium, Large and Extra Large are most commonly available.

FRESHNESS

How recently an egg was laid has a bearing on freshness, but the temperature at which it is held, the humidity and handling, also play their part. An egg one week old, held under ideal conditions, can be fresher than an egg left at room temperature for a day.

CARTON DATES

Egg cartons for USDA-inspected plants must display a Julian date — the date the eggs were packed. Although not required, they may also carry an expiration date beyond which the eggs should not be sold. In USDA-inspected plants, this date cannot exceed 30 days after the pack date. Plants not under USDA inspection are governed by the laws of their states.

Cooking with Eggs: Eggs can be cooked in myriad ways. Simply boiled, fried, or poached, they make a wonderful breakfast dish. Lightly cooked poached eggs are also delicious served as a lunch dish with high-fiber lentils or beans. Eggs are delicious baked, either on their own, with a drizzle of cream, or broken into a nest of lightly cooked bell peppers or leeks. They make delicious omelets, whether cooked

undisturbed until just softly set, combined with tomatoes and bell peppers to make an Italian frittata, or cooked with diced potato and onions to make the classic Spanish omelet. They are also often used as a filling for pies, savory tarts, and quiches.

Eggs are not only used in savory dishes. They are essential to many sweet dishes, too. They are added to cake, crêpe and popover batter, are crucial to meringues, mousses, and hot and cold soufflés, and are used in all kinds of desserts, from ice creams and custards to rice pudding.

When separated, egg yolks are used to thicken sauces and soups, giving them a rich, smooth consistency, while egg whites can be whisked to make meringues and soufflés. Use eggs at room temperature and remove them from the refrigerator about 30 minutes before cooking.

> ### Misleading Labels
> Eggs are often described with phrases such as "farm fresh", "natural," or "country-fresh," which conjure up images of hens roaming around in the open, but they may well refer to eggs that are laid by birds reared in indoor systems. Organic or free-range eggs will always be labeled as such.

Buying and Storing: Freshness is paramount when buying eggs. Buy from a store that has a high turnover of stock. You should reject any eggs that have a broken, dirty, or damaged shell. Most eggs are date stamped, but you can easily check if an egg is fresh by placing it in a bowl of cold water: if the egg sinks and lays flat it is fresh. The older the egg, the more it will stand on its end. A really old egg will actually float and shouldn't be eaten. Store eggs in a box in the main part of the fridge and not in a rack in the door as this can expose them to odors and damage. The shells are extremely porous, so eggs can be tainted by strong smells. Eggs should be stored large-end up for no longer than 3 weeks.

Health Benefits: Eggs have received much adverse publicity owing to their high cholesterol levels. However, attention has moved away from dietary cholesterol to cholesterol that is produced in the body from saturated fats. Saturated fats are now claimed to play a bigger role in raising cholesterol levels, and as eggs are low in saturated fat, they have been somewhat reprieved. They should, however, be eaten in moderation, and people with raised cholesterol levels should take particular care. Nutritionists recommend that we eat no more than four eggs a week. Eggs provide B vitamins, especially B_{12}, vitamins A and D, iron, choline, and phosphorus, and cooking does not significantly alter their nutritional content.

Quick Ideas for Eggs

• Brush beaten egg onto pastries and bread before baking to give them a golden glaze.
• For a protein boost, top Thai- or Chinese-flavored rice or noodle dishes with strips of thin omelet.
• Turn mixed salad greens into a light supper dish by adding a soft-cooked egg and some half-fat mayonnaise.
• For a simple dessert, make a soufflé omelet. Separate 2 eggs and whisk the whites and yolks separately. Fold together and add a little sugar. Cook in the same way as a non-sweet omelet and serve plain or fill with fruit conserve or lemon curd.

Herb Omelet

A simple, herb-flavored omelet is quick to cook and, served with a salad and a chunk of crusty bread, makes a nutritious, light meal. Even if you are going to serve more than one, it is better to cook individual omelets and eat them as soon as they are ready.

INGREDIENTS

2 eggs
1 tablespoon chopped fresh herbs, such as tarragon, parsley, or chives
1 teaspoon butter
salt and freshly ground black pepper

SERVES 1

1 Lightly beat the eggs in a bowl, add the fresh herbs, and season to taste.

2 Melt the butter in a heavy-based, non-stick skillet and swirl it around to coat the base evenly.

3 Pour in the egg mixture and, as the egg sets, push the edges toward the center using a spoon, allowing the raw egg to run on to the hot skillet.

4 Cook for about 2 minutes, without stirring, until the egg is just lightly set. Quickly fold over the omelet and serve at once.

The Pantry

The following section features a diverse range of foods that can enrich and add variety to a vegetarian diet. Some ingredients may be familiar, others less so, but all are useful to keep in the pantry. Each of the mentioned foods comes with notes on choosing, storage, and preparation, when necessary, as well as nutritional or medicinal properties.

Nuts

With the exception of peanuts, nuts are the fruits of trees. The quality and availability of fresh nuts varies with the seasons, although most types are sold dried, either whole or prepared ready for use. Shelled nuts come in many forms: they may be whole, blanched, halved, sliced, shredded, chopped, ground, or toasted.

Chestnuts

ALMONDS

There are two types of almond: sweet and bitter. The best sweet varieties are the flat and slender Jordan almonds from Spain. Heart-shaped Valencia almonds from Portugal and Spain, and the flatter Californian almonds are also widely available. For the best flavor, buy shelled almonds in their skins and blanch them yourself: cover with boiling water, leave for a few minutes, then drain, and the skins will peel off easily. Almonds are available ready-blanched, slivered, and ground. The latter adds a richness to cakes, tarts, pastry, and sauces. Bitter almonds are much smaller and are used in almond oil and essence. They should not be eaten raw as they contain traces of the lethal prussic acid.

BRAZIL NUTS

These are, in fact, seeds, and are grown mainly in the Amazon regions of Brazil and other neighboring countries. Between 12 and 20 Brazil nuts grow, packed snugly together, in a large brown husk, hence their three-cornered wedge shape. Brazil

nuts have a sweet, milky taste and are used mainly as dessert nuts. They have a high fat content, so go rancid very quickly.

CASHEW NUTS

These are the seeds of the "cashew apple"—an evergreen tree with bright-orange fruit. Cashew nuts have a sweet flavor and crumbly texture. They make delicious nut butters, or can be sprinkled into stir-fries or over salads. They are never sold in the shell and undergo an extensive heating process that removes the seed from its outer casing.

CHESTNUTS

Raw chestnuts are not recommended as they are not only unpleasant to eat but also contain tannic acid, which inhibits the absorption of iron. Most chestnuts are imported from France and Spain and they are excellent after roasting, which complements their soft, mealy texture. Unlike other nuts, they contain very little fat. Out of season, chestnuts can be bought dried, canned, or puréed.

Blanched, whole and shelled almonds; shelled cashew nuts (in bowl); shelled and whole Brazil nuts

Add whole chestnuts to winter stews, soups, stuffings, or pies. The sweetened purée is delicious in desserts.

COCONUTS

This versatile nut grows all over the tropics. The white dense meat, or flesh, is made into shredded coconut, blocks of creamed coconut, and a thick and creamy milk. A popular ingredient in Asian, African, and South American cuisines, coconut lends a sweet, creamy flavor to desserts,

Macadamia nuts

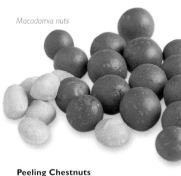

Peeling Chestnuts

Peeling chestnuts can be awkward and time-consuming but this is one of the simplest and quickest methods.

1 Place the chestnuts in a saucepan of boiling water, turn off the heat, and let stand for 5 minutes.

2 Remove the nuts with a slotted spoon, then leave until cool enough to handle. Peel with a sharp knife.

curries, soups, and casseroles. Use coconut in moderation, as it is particularly high in fat.

HAZELNUTS

Grown in the United States, Britain, Turkey, Italy, and Spain, hazelnuts are usually sold dried, and can be bought whole, shelled, and ground. They can be eaten raw, and the shelled nuts are especially good toasted. Hazelnuts can be grated or chopped for use in cakes and desserts, but they are also tasty in savory dishes and can be added to salads, stir-fries and pasta.

MACADAMIA NUTS

This round nut, about the size of a large hazelnut, is native to Australia, but is now grown in California and South America. Macadamia nuts are commonly sold shelled (the shell is extremely hard to crack). They have a crisp texture, a rich, buttery flavor and a high fat content.

Hazelnuts

Coconut Milk

Coconut milk or cream can be bought in cans or long-life cartons, but it is easy to make at home: put 2⅔ cups shredded coconut into a food processor, add scant 2 cups boiling water, and process for 30 seconds. Let cool slightly, then transfer to a cheesecloth-lined strainer placed over a bowl, and gather the ends of the cloth. Twist the cloth to extract the liquid, then discard the spent coconut. Store any unused coconut milk in the fridge for 1–2 days, or freeze.

Thick coconut cream, coconut milk, and shredded coconut

PEANUTS

Not strictly a nut but a
member of the pulse family,
peanuts bury themselves just
below the earth after flowering—
hence their alternative name,
groundnuts. They are a staple
food in many countries,
and are widely used in
Southeast Asia, notably for
satay sauce, and in African
cuisines, where they are used as an
ingredient in stews. In the West,
peanuts are a popular snack food; the
shelled nuts are frequently sold roasted
and salted, and they are used to make
peanut butter. Peanuts are particularly high
in fat and should be eaten in moderation.

Pecan nuts

Peanuts

Pine nuts

PECAN NUTS

A glossy, reddish-brown, oval-shaped shell
encloses the pecan kernel, which looks like
an elongated walnut, but has a sweeter,
milder flavor. This native American nut is a
favorite in sweet pies, especially the classic
pecan pie, but is also good eaten on its
own, or added to salads. However, pecan
nuts should be
eaten only as an
occasional treat because they have the
highest fat content of any nut, with a
calorie content to match.

PINE NUTS

These tiny, cream-colored nuts are the
fruit of the Mediterranean stone pine
tree. They have a rich, aromatic flavor,
which lends itself to toasting. Buy in small
quantities as their high oil content quickly
turns them rancid. Pine nuts are a key
ingredient in Italian pesto sauce, where
they are pounded with garlic, olive oil, and
basil, and in the Middle Eastern
sauce, tarator, in which
toasted pine nuts are
combined with bread,
garlic, milk, and olive oil to
make a creamy paste that has
a similar consistency to hummus.

PISTACHIO NUTS

Incredibly irresistible when served as
a snack, pistachio nuts have pale green
flesh and thin, reddish-purple skin. Sold
shelled or in a split shell, these mild nuts
are often used chopped as a colorful
garnish, sprinkled over both sweet and
non-sweet foods. Pistachio nuts have a
wonderful flavor; they are good in all
manner of desserts and can be made into

Making Nut Butter

Store-bought nut butters often contain
unwanted hydrogenated oil and can be
loaded with sugar. To avoid additives, make
your own butter using a combination of
peanuts, hazelnuts, and cashew nuts.

1 Place ½ cup shelled nuts in a food
processor or blender and process until
finely and evenly ground.

2 Pour 1–2 tablespoons sunflower oil
into the processor or blender and
process to a coarse paste. Store in an
airtight jar.

Walnuts

Nut Allergy

Any food has the potential to cause an allergic reaction, but peanuts, as well as walnuts, Brazil nuts, hazelnuts, and almonds are known to be common allergens. In cases of extreme allergy, nuts can trigger a life-threatening reaction known as anaphylaxis. Symptoms include facial swelling, shortness of breath, dizziness, and loss of consciousness, so it is essential that sufferers take every precaution to avoid nuts.

a delicious ice cream. They are widely used in Turkish and Arabic candies, notably nougat and Turkish Delight. Check before buying pistachio nuts for cooking, as they are often sold salted.

WALNUTS

Most walnuts are grown in France, Italy, and California, but they are also grown in the Middle East, Britain, and China. This versatile nut has been around for hundreds of years. When picked young, walnuts are referred to as "wet" and have fresh, milky-white kernels, which can be eaten raw, but are often pickled.

Dried walnuts have a delicious bitter-sweet flavor and can be bought shelled, chopped, or ground. They can be used to make excellent cakes and cookies, as well as rich pie fillings, but are also good added to non-sweet dishes, such as stir-fries and salads—the classic Waldorf salad combines whole kernels with sliced celery and apples in a mayonnaise dressing.

Buying and Storing:

Always buy nuts in small quantities from a store with a high turnover of stock, because if kept for too long, they can turn rancid. Nuts in their shells should feel heavy for their size. Store nuts in airtight containers in a cool, dark place or in the fridge and they should keep fresh for at least 3 months. When buying a coconut, make sure that there is no sign of mold or a rancid smell. Give it a shake—it should be full of liquid. Keep coconut milk in the fridge or freezer once opened. Shredded coconut can be stored in an airtight container, but don't keep it too long, as its high fat content means that it is prone to rancidity.

Health Benefits: Rich in B complex vitamins, vitamin E, potassium, magnesium, calcium, phosphorus, and iron, nuts offer the vegetarian an abundance of nutrients, although they contain a hefty number of calories. Most nuts are rich in monounsaturated and polyunsaturated fats, with the exception of Brazil nuts and coconuts, which are high in saturated fat, but do not contain cholesterol. Numerous studies highlight the substantial

health benefits of walnuts. According to one study, the essential fatty acids found in walnuts can decrease cholesterol levels and may reduce the risk of heart disease by 50 percent. Almonds and hazelnuts have similar properties.

Of all foods, Brazil nuts are the richest in selenium, which is a known mood enhancer. Apparently, a single Brazil nut each day will ensure that you are never deficient in this vital mineral.

Nuts are one of the richest vegetable sources of the antioxidant vitamin E, which has been associated with a lower risk of heart disease, stroke, and certain cancers.

Roasting and Skinning Nuts

The flavor of most nuts, particularly hazelnuts and peanuts, is improved by roasting. It also enables the thin outer skin to be removed more easily.

1 Place the nuts in a single layer on a cookie sheet. Bake in a preheated oven at 350°F for 10–20 minutes, or until the skins begin to split and the nuts are golden.

2 Put the nuts on to a dish cloth and rub to loosen and remove the skins.

Pistachio nuts

Seeds

They may look very small and unassuming, but seeds are nutritional powerhouses, packed with vitamins and minerals, as well as beneficial oils and protein. They can be used in a huge array of sweet and non-sweet dishes, and will add an instant, healthy boost, pleasant crunch, and nutty flavor when added to rice and pasta dishes, salads, stir-fries, soups, and yogurt.

SESAME SEEDS

These tiny, white or black seeds are a feature of Middle Eastern and Asian cooking. In the Middle East they are ground into tahini, a thick paste that is a key component of hummus. Sesame seeds are also ground to make halvah, a sweet confection from Greece, Israel, and Turkey. Gomassio, or gomashio, is the name of a crushed sesame seed condiment used in Japan. It can easily be made at home: toast the seeds, then crush with a little sea salt in a mortar using a pestle. Try a ratio of one part salt to five parts sesame seeds.

The flavor of sesame seeds is improved by roasting them in a dry skillet; it gives them a distinctive nuttiness. The toasted seeds make a good addition to salads and noodle dishes. Unroasted seeds can be used as a topping for breads, rolls, cakes, and cookies, and they can be added to pie dough.

When buying sesame seeds, try to find seeds that have been mechanically rolled—the tell-tale sign is a flat appearance. Seeds subjected to other methods of processing, such as salt-brining or a chemical bath, are usually glossy. Salt brining can affect the flavor of the seeds, as can chemical processing, which also damages their nutritional value.

SUNFLOWER SEEDS

These are the seeds of the sunflower, a symbol of summer and an important crop throughout the world. The impressive, golden-yellow flowers are grown for their seeds and oil; the leaves are used to treat malaria, and the stalks are made into fertilizer. Rich in vitamin E, the pale-green, tear-drop-shaped seeds have a semi-crunchy texture and an oily taste that is

Tahini (left) and black and white sesame seeds

much improved by dry-roasting. Sprinkle sunflower seeds over salads, rice pilaffs, and couscous, or use in bread dough, muffins, casseroles, and baked dishes.

POPPY SEEDS

These are the seeds of the opium poppy, but without any of the habit-forming alkaloids. Poppy seeds can be blue (usually described as black) or white. The black variety looks good sprinkled over cakes and breads, adding a pleasant crunch.

Sunflower seeds

Black and white poppy seeds

Black poppy seeds can be used to
make delicious seed cakes and
sweet breads, and they are
used in German and Eastern
European pastries, strudels,
and tarts. In India, the
ground white seeds are
used to thicken sauces, adding
a nutty flavor.

Pumpkin seeds

PUMPKIN SEEDS

Richer in iron than any other seed and an
excellent source of zinc, pumpkin seeds
make a nutritious snack eaten on their
own. They are also delicious lightly
toasted, tossed in a little toasted sesame
seed oil or soy sauce, and stirred into
mixed salad greens or rice salad. Pumpkin
seeds are widely used in South American
cooking, where they are generally roasted
and ground to make into sauces.

Quick Ideas for Seeds

• Sprinkle over breads, cakes, and
cookies just before baking.
• Combine with dried or fresh fruit,
chopped nuts and unsweetened
yogurt to make a nutritious breakfast.
• Add to flapjacks, whole wheat
biscuits, and pastry to give them a
nutty flavor.
• Add a spoonful of seeds to rissoles,
vegetable burgers, or casseroles.
• Mix with rolled oats, flour, butter or
margarine, and sugar to make a sweet
crumble topping. Omit the sugar to
make a non-sweet topping and
combine with chopped fresh herbs.
• Use sunflower or pumpkin seeds in
place of pine nuts to make pesto.
• Scatter over mixed salad greens.
• Add a nutritional boost to stir-fries
or noodle dishes, by scattering seeds
over them.

HEMP SEEDS

The cultivation of hemp has a long history,
but for various reasons it fell out of
fashion. Today, hemp is making a comeback
as a food. Hemp seeds are best roasted as
this enhances their nutty flavor, and they
can be used in a variety of sweet and non-
sweet dishes.

LINSEEDS

Linseed oil has long been used to
embellish wooden furniture. However, the
golden seed, also known as flaxseed, is a
rich source of polyunsaturated fat,
including the essential fatty acid, linoleic
acid. Linseeds can be added to muesli and
other breakfast cereals, mixed into bread
dough, or sprinkled over salads.

Buying and Storing: Seeds are best bought
in small quantities from stores with a high
turnover of stock. Purchase whole seeds,
rather than ground, and store them in a
cool, dark place as they are prone to
turning rancid. After opening the packet,
transfer the seeds to an airtight container.

Linseeds (left) and hemp seeds

Health Benefits: Seeds contain valuable
amounts of the antioxidant vitamin
E, which enhances the immune
system and protects cells from
oxidation. Vitamin E also
improves blood circulation,
and promotes healing and
normal blood clotting, as
well as reducing infections
associated with aging. Numerous
studies show that the vitamin
works in tandem with beta carotene
and vitamin C to fight off certain cancers
and heart disease as well as slowing the
progression of Alzheimer's disease.

Seeds, particularly sunflower seeds, may
help to reduce blood cholesterol levels in
the body because they contain plentiful
amounts of linoleic acid, which is also
known as omega-6 fatty acid.

For their size, seeds contain a huge
amount of iron. Sesame seeds are
particularly rich—2–3 tablespoons
provide nearly half the daily requirement
of iron, and ½ cup pumpkin seeds provides
almost three-quarters of the iron we
need each day. Sunflower seeds are often
prescribed by natural medicine
practitioners for their restorative qualities.

Roasting Seeds

The flavor of seeds is much improved by
"roasting" them in a dry skillet. Black
poppy seeds won't turn golden brown, so
watch them carefully to make sure that
they don't scorch.

1 Spread out a spoonful or two of seeds
in a thin layer in a large, non-stick skillet
and heat gently.

2 Cook over medium heat for
2–3 minutes, tossing the seeds
frequently, until they are golden brown.

Spices

Highly revered for thousands of years, spices—the seeds, fruit, pods, bark, and buds of plants—have been the reason for wars and were sometimes traded as a currency. In addition to their ability to add flavor and interest to the most unassuming of ingredients, the evocative aroma of spices stimulates the appetite. Today, spices are still prized for their medicinal properties and culinary uses, and they play a vital role in healthy and appetizing vegetarian cooking.

Caraway seeds

Ground allspice

ALLSPICE

These small, dried berries of a tropical, South American tree have a sweet, warming flavor reminiscent of a blend of cloves, cinnamon, and nutmeg. Although allspice is available ready-ground, it is best to buy the spice whole to retain its flavor, and grind just before use in cakes and cookies. The whole berries can be added to marinades or mulled wine. Allspice is used to relieve digestive problems, including flatulence.

CARAWAY

An important flavoring in Eastern European, Austrian, and German cooking, caraway seeds are sprinkled over rye bread, cakes, and cookies. They have a distinctive, sweet, aniseed flavor, which is also a welcome addition to potato- and cheese-based dishes, steamed carrots, or cabbage. Caraway is recommended for colicky babies and has a similar effect in adults, relieving gas and aiding digestion. It can also be used to relieve menstrual pain.

CARDAMOM

Often used in Middle Eastern and Indian cooking, cardamom is best bought whole in its pod as it soon loses its aromatic flavor when ground. The pod can be used whole, slightly crushed, or for a more intense flavor, the seeds can be

Cardamom pods

ground. Cardamom is superb in both sweet and non-sweet dishes. It can be infused in milk used to flavor rice pudding or ice cream, and is often added to curries and other Indian dishes. The seeds can be chewed whole to freshen the breath and calm indigestion. Colds and coughs are also said to be relieved by eating cardamom.

CAYENNE

This fiery, reddish-brown powder adds color and heat, rather than flavor, to curries, soups, and stews. It comes from the ground pod and seeds of a very pungent variety of chile pepper, *Capsicum frutescens*, and is sometimes referred to as red pepper. Cayenne possesses stimulant, antiseptic, and digestive properties. It can improve blood circulation, but if eaten in large quantities may aggravate the stomach. A more unusual use of cayenne is to sprinkle it in your shoes to warm up cold feet!

Cayenne, celery seeds, chile powder, and chile flakes.

Above, clockwise from left: Cinnamon sticks, coriander seeds, cloves, and ground cinnamon

CELERY SEEDS

These tiny brown seeds have a similar flavor to celery, but are more highly aromatic. It is important to grind or crush them before use to avoid any bitterness. Celery seeds can be used in almost any dish that calls for celery, and they add a pungent flavor to vegetarian bakes, stews, soups, sauces, and egg dishes. Celery salt is a mixture of ground celery seeds, salt, and other herbs. Celery seeds are carminative, relieving both flatulence and indigestion.

CHILE

Fresh chile peppers are covered in the vegetable section, but this versatile spice is also sold in dried, powdered, and flaked form. Dried chiles tend to be hotter than fresh, and this is certainly true of chile flakes, which contain both the seeds and the flesh. The best pure chile powders do not contain added ingredients, such as onion and garlic. A powerful stimulant and expectorant, chile also has a reputation as an aphrodisiac.

CINNAMON

This warm, comforting spice is available in sticks (quills) and ground. As the bark is difficult to grind, it is useful to keep both forms in the pantry. Cinnamon can enhance both sweet and non-sweet dishes. Use the sticks to flavor pilaffs, curries, couscous, and dried fruit compotes, but remove before serving. Ground cinnamon adds a pleasing fragrance to cakes, cookies, and fruit. Cinnamon is an effective detoxifier and cleanser, containing substances that kill bacteria and other microorganisms.

CLOVES

The unopened bud of an evergreen tree from Southeast Asia, this spice is often used in combination with cinnamon to flavor desserts, cakes, and cookies. Cloves are often used to flavor the syrup when poaching oranges, but they are also delicious with cooked apples.

Clove oil has long been used as a cure for toothache, and both its antiseptic and anesthetic qualities can relieve other pains.

CORIANDER

Alongside cumin, ground coriander is a key ingredient in Indian curry powders and garam masala, and in northern Europe the ivory-colored seeds are used as a pickling spice. Coriander seeds have a sweet, earthy, burnt-orange flavor that is more pronounced than the fresh leaves. The ready-ground powder rapidly loses its flavor and aroma, so it is best to buy whole seeds, which are easily ground in a mortar using a pestle, or in a coffee grinder. Before grinding, lightly dry-roast the seeds in a skillet to enhance their flavor. Coriander has been prescribed as a digestive for thousands of years, relieving indigestion, diarrhea, and nausea. It also has antibacterial properties.

Cumin seeds, ground cumin, and (front) fenugreek

CUMIN

Extensively used in Indian curries, cumin is also a familiar component of Mexican, North African, and Middle Eastern cooking. The seeds have a robust aroma and slightly bitter taste, which is tempered by dry-roasting. Black cumin seeds, which are also known as nigella, are milder and sweeter. Ground cumin can be harsh, so it is best to buy the whole seeds and grind them just before use to ensure a fresh flavor. Cumin is good in tomato- or grain-based dishes, and its digestive properties mean that it is also ideal with beans.

Fresh ginger root

GINGER

This spice is probably one of the oldest and most popular herbal medicines. The fresh root, which is spicy, peppery, and fragrant, is good in both sweet and non-sweet dishes, adding a hot, yet refreshing, flavor to marinades, stir-fries, soups, curries, grains, and fresh vegetables. It also adds warmth to poached fruit, pastries, and cakes. Ground ginger is the usual choice for flavoring cakes, cookies, and other baked goods, but finely grated fresh ginger can also be used and is equally good.

Ground ginger

FENUGREEK

This spice is commonly used in commercial curry powders, along with cumin and coriander. On its own though, fenugreek should be used in moderation because its bitter-sweet flavor, which is mellowed by dry-frying, can be quite overpowering. The seeds have a hard shell and are difficult to grind, but they can be sprouted and make a good addition to mixed salad greens and bean salads, as well as sandwich fillings. Fenugreek has long been prescribed to treat stomach and intestinal disorders, and its ability to cleanse the body may help in the release of toxins.

Ginger tea, made by steeping a few slices of fresh ginger root in hot water for a few minutes, can calm and soothe the stomach after a bout of food poisoning, as well as ward off colds and flu.

Pink pickled ginger

This pretty, finely sliced ginger pickle is served as an accompaniment to Japanese food and is used to flavor sushi rice.

Crystallized ginger

Preserved in a thick sugar syrup and sold in jars, this sweet ginger can be chopped and used in desserts, or added to cake mixtures, steamed puddings, cookies, shortbread, and muffins.

Buying and Storing: Fresh ginger root should look firm, thin-skinned, and unblemished. Avoid withered, woody-looking roots as these are likely to be dry and fibrous. Store in the fridge. Ground ginger should smell aromatic; keep in a cool, dark place.

Preparing Fresh Ginger

1 Fresh ginger root is most easily peeled using a vegetable peeler or a small, sharp paring knife.

3 Grate ginger finely—special graters can be found in Asian stores, but a box grater will do the job equally well.

2 Chop ginger, using a sharp knife, to the size specified in the recipe.

4 Freshly grated ginger can be squeezed to release the juice.

using a pestle. Bottled, chopped lemongrass and lemongrass purée are also available. Lemongrass is reputed to benefit rheumatism.

Galangal

GALANGAL

Closely related to ginger, fresh galangal looks similar but has a reddish-brown or cream-colored skin. It was popular in England during the Middle Ages, but fell out of favor. With the increased interest in Southeast Asian cooking, this knobby root is again widely available and can be found in Asian stores. Its fragrant, slightly peppery taste can be overpowering if used in excess. Avoid the powdered version, as it is nothing like the fresh. Prepare the root in the same way as ginger: peel, then slice,

Pink pickled ginger

Health Benefits: The health benefits of ginger have been well documented for centuries. Recent studies confirm that ginger can successfully prevent nausea and may be more effective than prescribed drugs. Research also shows ginger to be effective in the treatment of pain and gastrointestinal disorders, and it may even halt certain cancers.

LEMONGRASS

This long fibrous stalk has a fragrant citrus aroma and flavor when cut and is a familiar part of Southeast Asian and particularly Thai cooking, where it is used in coconut-flavored curries. If you have difficulty finding lemongrass, lemon rind is a suitable alternative, but it lacks the distinctive flavor of the fresh stalks.

To use, remove the tough, woody outer layers, trim the root, then cut off the lower 2 inches, and slice into thin rounds or pound in a mortar

grate, or pound in a mortar using a pestle. Galangal has similar medicinal properties to ginger, relieving nausea and stomach problems.

MUSTARD

There are three different types of mustard seed: white, brown, and black, which is the most pungent. The flavor and aroma is only apparent when the seeds are

crushed or mixed with liquid. If fried in a little oil before use, the flavor of the seeds is improved. As the intensity of mustard diminishes with both time and cooking; it is best added to dishes toward the end of cooking, or just before the dish is served.

Like many hot spices, mustard is traditionally used as a stimulant, cleansing the body of toxins and helping to ward off colds and flu.

Above: American mustard, Dijon mustard, wholegrain mustard, mustard powder, and black and white mustard seeds

Lemongrass

NUTMEG AND MACE

When it is picked, the nutmeg seed is surrounded by a lacy membrane called mace. Both are dried and used as spices. Nutmeg and mace taste similar, and their warm, sweet flavor enlivens white sauces, cheese-based dishes, and vegetables, as well as custards, cakes, and cookies. Freshly grated nutmeg is far superior to the ready-ground variety, which loses its flavor and aroma with time. Although it is a hallucinogen if eaten in excess, when consumed in the small quantities that are needed in recipes, nutmeg improves both appetite and digestion.

White, black, and pink peppercorns

Ground saffron and saffron threads

ground in a peppermill when you need them because they quickly lose their aroma.

White pepper

This has a less aromatic flavor than black pepper and is generally used in white sauces and other dishes to avoid dark specks of black pepper.

PEPPER

Undoubtedly the oldest, most widely used spice in the world, pepper was as precious as gold and silver in medieval Europe. It is a very useful seasoning, because it not only adds flavor of its own to a dish, but also brings out the flavor of the other ingredients. Pepper is a digestive stimulant, as well as a decongestant and antioxidant.

Black peppercorns

These are the dried green berries of the vine pepper and they are relatively mild. Black peppercorns are best when freshly

Right, clockwise from top left: Pumpkin pie spice, ground and whole nutmegs, and paprika

Green peppercorns

These unripened berries have a milder flavor than black or white peppercorns and may be dried or preserved in brine. They are sometimes used to make a spicy peppercorn sauce.

Pink peppercorns

These pretty, pink berries are not a true pepper. They are the processed berry of a type of poison ivy and should be used in small amounts as they are mildly toxic.

PAPRIKA

Paprika is a milder relative of cayenne and can be used more liberally, adding flavor as well as heat. Like cayenne, it is a digestive stimulant and has antiseptic properties. Paprika can also improve blood circulation, but if eaten in large quantities may aggravate the stomach.

SAFFRON

The world's most expensive spice is made from the dried stigmas of *Crocus salivus*. Only a tiny amount of this bright-orange spice is needed to add a wonderful color and delicate bitter-sweet flavor to rice, stews, soups, and milky puddings. Saffron has the ability to calm and balance the body and is believed to be an aphrodisiac.

Ground and fresh turmeric

Grinding Spices

Whole spices ground by hand provide the best flavor and aroma. Grind as you need them and do not be tempted to grind too much, as they tend to lose their potency and flavor. Some spices, such as mace, fenugreek, cloves, turmeric, and cinnamon, are difficult to grind at home and are better bought ready-ground.

Grind whole spices in a mortar using a pestle—or use an electric coffee grinder if desired.

Toasting Spices

This process enhances the flavor and aroma of spices and is thought to make them more digestible.

Put the spices in a dry skillet and cook over low heat, shaking the skillet frequently, for 1 minute, or until the spices release their aroma.

TURMERIC

Sometimes used as an alternative to saffron, turmeric delivers a similar yellow color but has a very different flavor. It adds an earthy, peppery flavor to curries and stews. Turmeric is valued for its antibacterial and antifungal qualities. It can aid digestion and in Asia it is believed to be a remedy for liver problems.

VANILLA

These slender, chocolate-brown beans have a fragrant, exotic aroma and luscious, almost creamy flavor. They can be used more than once; simply rinse and dry before storing in an airtight jar. Buy natural vanilla extract or essence, which is made by infusing the beans in alcohol; artificial vanilla flavoring is nowhere near so good. Vanilla is considered to be an aphrodisiac and a tonic for the brain.

Buying and Storing: Buy spices in small quantities from a store with a regular turnover of stock. Aroma is the best indication of freshness, as this diminishes when the spice is stale. Store in airtight jars in a cool place away from direct light.

Natural vanilla extract and vanilla pods

Salt

Moderate amounts of salt are needed by the body, but it is easy to consume too much, as salt is added to many processed foods. Too much salt can lead to high blood pressure, hypertension, water retention and may increase the risk of heart disease. Used in small amounts, salt can enhance the flavor of food. Use rock or sea salt rather than refined table salt.

Table salt (top), rock salt (right), and sea salt

Pasta

Once considered a fattening food, pasta is now recognized as an important part of a healthy diet. The variety of shapes is almost endless, from the myriad tiny soup pastas to huge shells used for stuffing. Pasta can be plain, made with egg, or flavored with ingredients such as tomato or spinach. Low in fat and high in complex carbohydrates, it provides plenty of long-term energy. Corn and buckwheat varieties are also available, as is whole wheat pasta, which is high in fiber.

Spaghetti, linguine, and tagliatelle

Pasta is one of our simplest, yet most versatile foods. A combination of wheat flour and water produces the basic dough, which can then be formed into an infinite number of shape variations. Alter the type of flour, add fresh eggs or a vegetable purée, and the options are even greater. Although pasta is itself a low-fat food, it is important to take care when choosing the accompanying sauce, as overloading on cheese or cream can soon transform pasta into a high-fat food.

DURUM WHEAT PASTA

This is the most readily available type of pasta and can be made with or without egg. Plain wheat pasta is used for straight long shapes, such as spaghetti, while long shapes made with egg pasta, because it is more delicate, are traditionally packed in nests or compressed into waves. Lasagne can be made with either plain or egg pasta. At one time, almost all short pasta shapes were made from plain pasta, but shapes made with egg pasta are becoming increasingly available. Pasta made with egg has several advantages over plain pasta: it is more nutritious, many people consider it to have a superior flavor, and it is more difficult to overcook.

COLORED AND FLAVORED PASTA

A variety of ingredients can be added to the pasta dough to give it both flavor and color. The most common additions are tomato and spinach, but beet, saffron, fresh herbs, such as basil, and even chocolate are used. Mixed bags of pasta are also available—the traditional combination of plain and spinach-flavored

Buckwheat pasta spirals and short-cut pizzoccheri

Right: Corn or maize pasta can be bought in a wide variety of shapes, from simple elbow macaroni to fusilli and three-colored radiatori

pasta is called paglia e fieno, which means straw and hay. However, there are many other mixtures, some having as many as seven different flavors and colors of pasta.

WHOLE WHEAT PASTA

This substantial pasta is made from whole wheat flour and contains more fiber than plain durum wheat pasta. It has a slightly chewy texture and nutty flavor and takes longer to cook. Whole wheat spaghetti (bigoli), a traditional Italian variety that comes from the area around Venice known as the Veneto, can be found in good Italian delicatessens, and in health-food stores and supermarkets. There is an increasing range of wholewheat shapes, from tiny soup pastas to rotelle (wheels) and lasagne.

BUCKWHEAT PASTA

Pasta made from buckwheat flour has a nutty taste and is darker in color than whole wheat pasta. Pizzoccheri from Lombardy is the classic shape. These thin, flat noodles are traditionally sold in nests like tagliatelle (although pizzoccheri are about half the length), but they are also available cut into short strips.

Other buckwheat pasta shapes are available in health-food stores and supermarkets. Buckwheat pasta is gluten-free and suitable for people who are intolerant to gluten or wheat. It is also very nutritious, containing all eight amino acids, calcium, zinc, and B vitamins.

CORN PASTA

This pasta is made with corn or maize flour, is gluten-free, and is a good alternative pasta for people who cannot tolerate gluten or wheat. It is made in a wide range of shapes, including spaghetti, fusilli (spirals), and conchiglie (shells), as well as more unusual varieties. Plain corn pasta is a sunshine-yellow color, and may be flavored with spinach or tomato. It is cooked and used in the same way as wheat pasta and is available from many health-food stores and supermarkets.

PASTA SHAPES

Long pasta

Dried long pasta in the form of spaghetti is probably the best known, but there are many other varieties, from fine vermicelli to pappardelle—broad ribbon noodles. Tagliatelle, the most common form of ribbon noodles, is usually sold coiled into nests. Long pasta is best served with a thin sauce, made with olive oil, butter, cream, eggs, grated cheese, or chopped fresh herbs. When vegetables are added to the sauce, they should be finely chopped.

Fresh spaghetti, tagliatelle, and fettuccine are widely available.

Short pasta

There are hundreds of different short dried pasta shapes, which may be made with plain pasta dough or the more nutritious yellow, egg pasta. Short pasta isn't often sold fresh because most shapes

Above: Pasta can be colored and flavored in a variety of ways, but plain, spinach, and tomato varieties are the most popular

are difficult to produce, but you may find one or two in some Italian delicatessens, and a few fresh shapes are also available from larger supermarkets.

Conchiglie (shells) are one of the most useful shapes because they are concave and trap virtually any sauce. Fusilli (spirals) are good with thick tomato-based sauces and farfalle (butterflies) can be served with creamy sauces, but are very versatile and work equally well with tomato- or olive oil-based sauces. Macaroni used to be the most common short shape, and being hollow, it is good for most sauces and baked dishes. However, penne (quills) have become more popular, perhaps because the hollow tubes with diagonally cut ends

Spinach and whole wheat lasagne and plain cannelloni

go well with virtually any sauce. They are particularly good with chunky vegetable sauces or baked with cheese sauce.

Flat pasta

Lasagne is designed to be baked between layers of sauce, or cooked in boiling water, then layered, or rolled around a filling to make cannelloni. Lasagne is made from plain or egg pasta and both fresh and dried versions are available. The pasta sheets may be flavored with tomato or spinach, or made with whole wheat flour.

Stuffed pasta

The most common stuffed pasta shapes are ravioli, tortellini (little pies), and cappelletti (little hats), although there are other lesser-known shapes available from Italian delicatessens. Plain, spinach, and tomato doughs are the most usual, and there is a wide range of vegetarian fillings.

Pasta for soup

These tiny shapes are mostly made from plain durum wheat pasta, although you may find them with egg. There are hundreds of different ones, from tiny risi, which look like grains of rice, to alfabeti (alphabet shapes), which are popular with children. Slightly larger shapes, such as farfalline (little bows) and tubetti (little tubes), are used in thicker soups.

Buying and Storing: The quality of pasta varies tremendously—choose good-quality Italian brands of pasta made from 100 percent durum wheat, and visit your local Italian delicatessen to buy fresh pasta, rather than buying pre-packed pasta from the supermarket. Dried pasta will keep almost indefinitely, but if you transfer the pasta to a storage jar, it is a good idea to use up the remaining pasta before adding any from a new packet. Fresh pasta from a delicatessen is usually sold loose

---

Quick Ideas for Pasta

• To make a simple, but richly flavored tomato sauce: place some plum or cherry tomatoes in an ovenproof dish and drizzle with a little olive oil. Roast in a hot oven for 15 minutes, then add one or two peeled garlic cloves, and continue roasting for about 15 minutes more. Transfer to a food processor and blend with basil leaves. Season and stir into cooked pasta.

• Toss cooked pasta in a little chile oil, scatter with arugula leaves and pine nuts, and serve with finely grated Parmesan cheese.

• Stir a spoonful of black olive tapenade into cooked pasta, then scatter a few lightly toasted walnuts on top before serving.

• Roast a head of garlic, then squeeze out the puréed cloves, and mix with olive oil. Toss with cooked pasta and sprinkle with plenty of fresh, chopped flat leaf parsley.

• Olives, mushrooms, eggplant, and artichokes bottled in olive oil make quick and delicious additions to pasta.

• Combine cooked pasta with small chunks of mozzarella cheese, sliced sun-dried tomatoes, chopped fresh mint, and a splash of olive oil.

Large and small conchiglie (shells)

Choosing the Right Shape

While it is unnecessary to stick rigidly to hard-and-fast rules, some pasta shapes definitely work better than others with particular sauces.

• Long pasta shapes, such as spaghetti, linguine, tagliatelle, and fettuccine, suit smooth cream- or olive oil-based sauces, or vegetable sauces where the ingredients are very finely chopped.

• Hollow shapes, such as penne (quills), fusilli (spirals), and macaroni, all work well with more robust sauces, such as cheese, tomato, and vegetable.

• Stuffed pasta shapes, such as ravioli and cappelletti, are good with simple sauces made with butter, extra virgin olive oil, or tomatoes.

• In soups, the delicate small shapes, risi (rice), orzi (barley), and quadrucci (squares), suit lighter broths, while the more substantial conchigliette (little shells) and farfalline (little butterflies) go well in heartier vegetable soups.

Fresh tortellini

Health Benefits: Pasta provides the body with fuel for all kinds of physical activity, from running a marathon to walking to the bus stop. High in complex carbohydrates, pasta is broken down slowly, providing energy over a long period of time. Whole wheat pasta is the most nutritious, containing a richer concentration of vitamins, minerals, and fiber. Nevertheless, all pasta is a useful source of protein, as well as being low in fat. Buckwheat is very nutritious; it contains all eight essential amino acids, making it a complete protein. It is also particularly high in fiber.

Cooking Pasta

Pasta should be cooked in a large pan of boiling salted water to allow the strands or shapes to expand, and stirred occasionally to prevent them from sticking together. Do not add oil to the cooking water, as it makes the pasta slippery and prevents it from absorbing the sauce. Cooking instructions are given on the packaging, but always taste just before the end of the given time to prevent overcooking. Dried pasta should be *al dente*, or firm to the bite, while fresh pasta should be just tender.

Bring a large pan of salted water to a boil. For shapes, add the pasta and cover the pan. Bring quickly back to a boil and remove the lid. Reduce the heat slightly, then stir the pasta, and cook according to the packet instructions. For long straight pasta, such as spaghetti, coil the pasta into the water as it softens.

and is best cooked the same day, but can be kept in the fridge for a day or two. Fresh pasta from a supermarket is likely to be packed in plastic packs and bags, and these will keep for 3–4 days in the fridge. Fresh pasta freezes well and should be cooked from frozen. Packs and bags of supermarket pasta have the advantage of being easy to store in the freezer.

Above: Tiny soup pasta is available in hundreds of different shapes

Noodles

The fast food of the East, noodles can be made from wheat flour, rice, buckwheat flour, or mung bean flour. Both fresh and dried noodles are readily available in health-food stores and Asian stores as well as supermarkets. Like pasta, noodles are low in fat and high in complex carbohydrates, so provide long-term energy.

Rice noodles

WHEAT NOODLES

There are two main types of noodle: plain and egg. Plain noodles are made from strong flour and water. They can be flat or round and come in various thicknesses.

Udon noodles

These thick Japanese noodles can be round or flat and are available fresh, pre-cooked, or dried. Whole wheat udon noodles have a more robust flavor.

Somen noodles

Usually sold in bundles held together by a paper band, these thin, white noodles are available from Asian stores.

Egg noodles

Far more common than the plain wheat variety, egg noodles are sold both fresh and dried. The Chinese type come in various thicknesses. Very fine egg noodles, which resemble vermicelli, are usually sold in coils. Whole wheat egg noodles are widely available from larger supermarkets.

Ramen noodles

These Japanese egg noodles are also sold in coils and are often cooked and served with an accompanying broth.

RICE NOODLES

These fine, delicate noodles are made from rice and are opaque-white in color. Like wheat noodles, they come in various widths, from the very thin strands known as rice vermicelli, which are popular in Thailand and southern China, to the thicker rice sticks, which are used more in Vietnam and Malaysia. A huge range of rice noodles is available dried in Asian grocers, and fresh ones are occasionally found in the chiller cabinets. Since all rice noodles are pre-cooked, they need only to be soaked in hot water for a few minutes to soften them before use in stir-fries and salads.

Udon noodles (above) and cellophane noodles

CELLOPHANE VERMICELLI AND NOODLES

Made from mung bean starch, these translucent noodles, also known as bean thread vermicelli and glass noodles, come in a variety of thicknesses and are only available dried. Although very fine, the strands are firm and fairly tough. Cellophane noodles don't need to be boiled, and are simply soaked in boiling water for 10–15 minutes. They have a fantastic texture, which they retain when cooked, never becoming soggy. Cellophane noodles are almost tasteless unless combined with other strongly flavored foods and seasonings. They are never eaten on their own, but used as an ingredient. They are good in vegetarian dishes, and as an ingredient in spring rolls.

BUCKWHEAT NOODLES

Soba are the best-known type of buckwheat noodles. They are a much darker color than wheat noodles—almost brownish gray. In Japan, soba noodles are traditionally served in soups or stir-fries with a variety of sauces.

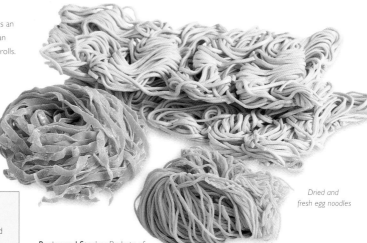

Dried and fresh egg noodles

Quick Ideas for Noodles
• To make a simple broth, dissolve mugi miso in hot water, add cooked soba noodles; sprinkle with chile flakes, and sliced scallions.

• Cook ramen noodles in vegetable stock, then add a splash of dark soy sauce, shredded spinach, and grated ginger (above). Serve sprinkled with sesame seeds and fresh cilantro.

• Stir-fry sliced shiitake and oyster mushrooms in garlic and ginger, then toss with rice or egg noodles (above). Scatter with fresh chives and a little toasted sesame oil.
• In a food processor, blend together some lemon grass, chile pepper, garlic, ginger, kaffir lime leaves, and fresh cilantro. Fry the paste in a little sunflower oil and combine with cooked ribbon noodles. Sprinkle fresh basil and chopped scallions on top before serving.

Buying and Storing: Packets of fresh noodles are found in the chiller cabinets of Asian stores. They usually carry a "use-by" date and must be stored in the fridge. Dried noodles will keep for many months if stored in an airtight container in a cool, dry place.

Health Benefits: Noodles are high in complex carbohydrates, which are broken down slowly, providing energy over a long period of time. Whole wheat noodles are the most nutritious, containing a richer concentration of vitamins, minerals, and fiber. Nevertheless, all noodles are a useful source of protein, as well as being low in fat. Buckwheat noodles are made from buckwheat flour, which contains all eight essential amino acids, making it a complete protein. It is also particularly high in fiber. Cellophane noodles are made from mung bean starch, which is reputed to be one of the most powerful detoxifiers.

Cooking Wheat Noodles

Wheat noodles are very easy to cook. Both dried and fresh noodles are cooked in a large pan of boiling water; how long depends on the type of noodle and the thickness of the strips. Dried noodles need about 3 minutes cooking time, while fresh ones will often be ready in less than a minute. Fresh noodles may need to be rinsed quickly in cold water to prevent them from overcooking.

Whole wheat egg noodles

Oils

There is a wide variety of cooking oils and they are produced from a number of different sources: from cereals such as corn; from fruits such as olives; from nuts such as walnuts, almonds, and hazelnuts; and from seeds such as canola, safflower, and sunflower. They can be extracted by simple mechanical means such as pressing or crushing, or by further processing, usually heating. Virgin oils, which are obtained from the first cold pressing of the olives, nuts, or seeds, are sold unrefined, and have the most characteristic flavor. They are also the most expensive.

OLIVE OIL

Indisputably the king of oils, olive oil varies in flavor and color, depending on how it is made and where it comes from. Climate, soil, harvesting, and pressing all influence the end result—generally, the hotter the climate, the more robust the oil. Thus oils from southern Italy, Greece, and Spain have a stronger flavor and a darker color than those from the rest of Italy and France. Olive oil is rich in monounsaturated fat, which has been found to reduce cholesterol, thereby reducing the risk of heart disease. There are different grades to choose from.

Extra virgin olive oil

This premium olive oil has a superior flavor. It comes from the first cold pressing of the olives and has a low acidity—less than 1 percent. Extra virgin olive oil is not recommended for frying, as heat impairs its flavor, but it is good in salad dressings, especially when combined with lighter oils. It is delicious as a sauce on its own, stirred into pasta with chopped garlic and black pepper, or drizzled onto steamed vegetables.

Virgin olive oil

Also a pure first-pressed oil, this has a slightly higher level of acidity than extra virgin olive oil, and can be used in much the same way.

Essential Fats

We all need some fat in our diet. It keeps us warm, adds flavor to our food, carries essential vitamins A, D, E, and K around the body, and provides essential fatty acids, which cannot be produced in the body, but are vital for growth and development, and may reduce the risk of heart attacks.

What is more important is the type and amount of fat that we eat. Some fats are better for us than others, and we should adjust our intake accordingly. It is recommended that fat should make up no more than 35 percent of our diet.

Extra virgin olive oil (left), sunflower oil (right), and safflower oil (far right)

Peanut oil (left) and almond oil

Pure olive oil

Refined and blended to remove impurities, this type of olive oil has a much lighter flavor than virgin or extra virgin olive oil and is suitable for all types of cooking. It can be used for shallow frying.

OTHER OILS

There is a wide range of light, processed oils on the market, which are all relatively taste-free and have a variety of uses in the kitchen.

Corn oil

One of the most economical and widely used vegetable oils, corn oil has a deep golden color and a fairly strong flavor. It is suitable for cooking and frying, but should not be used for salad dressings. Corn is rich in omega-6 (linoleic) fatty acids, which are believed to reduce harmful cholesterol in the body.

Safflower oil

This is a light, all-purpose oil, which comes from the seeds of the safflower. It can be used in place of sunflower and peanut oils, but is a little thicker and has a slightly stronger flavor. It is suitable for deep-frying, but is best used with other more strongly flavored ingredients, and is ideal for cooking spicy foods. Safflower oil contains more polyunsaturated fat than any other type of oil and it is low in saturated fat.

Sunflower oil

Perhaps the best all-purpose oil, sunflower oil is very light and almost tasteless. It is very versatile, and can be used for frying and in cooking, or to make salad dressings, when it can be combined with a stronger flavored oil, such as olive oil or walnut oil. Sunflower oil is extracted from the seeds of the sunflower. It is very high in polyunsaturated fat and low in saturated fat.

Soy oil

This neutral flavored, all-purpose oil, which is extracted from soybeans, is probably the most widely used oil in the world. It is useful for frying because it has a high smoking point, and remains stable at high temperatures. It is also widely used in margarines. It is rich in polyunsaturated and monounsaturated fats and low in saturates. Find a brand that is not made from genetically modified soybeans.

Peanut oil

Also known as groundnut oil, this relatively tasteless oil is useful for frying, cooking, and dressing salads. Chinese peanut oil is darker in color than other types and has a

Soy oil

Quick Ideas for Marinades

• Mix olive oil with chopped fresh herbs, such as parsley, chives, oregano, chervil, and basil. Add a splash or two of lemon juice and season with salt and pepper.

• Combine peanut oil, toasted sesame oil, dark soy sauce, sweet sherry, rice vinegar, and crushed garlic. Use as a marinade for bean curd or tempeh.

• Mix together olive oil, lemon juice, sherry, honey, and crushed garlic and use as a marinade for vegetable and halloumi kebabs.

more distinctive nutty flavor. It is good in Asian salads and stir-fries. Peanut oil has a higher percentage of monounsaturated fat than soy oil, but also contains polyunsaturated fat.

Canola oil

This bland-tasting, all-purpose oil, also known as rapeseed, can be used for frying, cooking, and in salad dressings. It contains a higher percentage of monounsaturated fat than any other oil, with the exception of olive oil.

Grapeseed oil

A delicate, mild-flavored oil, which does not impose on other ingredients, grapeseed oil is pressed from grape seeds left over from wine-making. It is good in cooking and for frying, and can be used to make salad dressings, especially when combined with a stronger flavored nut or olive oil. Grapeseed oil is high in poly-unsaturated fat.

Canola oil

SPECIALTY OILS

As well as the light, all-purpose oils that are used for everyday cooking, there are several richly flavored oils that are used in small quantities, often as a flavoring ingredient in salad dressings and marinades, rather than for cooking.

Sesame oil

There are two types of sesame oil—the pale and light version that is pressed from untoasted seeds, and the rich, dark, toasted oil that is used in Asian cuisines. The lighter oil, popular in India and the Middle East, has a mild flavor and a high smoking point, and is useful for cooking. Dark sesame oil, which has a wonderfully nutty aroma and taste, is useful for flavoring marinades and stir-fries. It has a much stronger taste than either walnut oil or olive oil and is too overpowering to use in large quantities. However, it can be mixed with milder oils, such as peanut or soy. Heating helps to intensify the aroma of toasted sesame oil, but it should never be heated for too long. Both types of sesame oil are high in polyunsaturated fat.

Walnut oil

This is an intensely flavored oil that is delicious in salad dressings and marinades, but shouldn't be used for frying as heat diminishes its rich taste (it is also far too expensive to use in any great quantity). Instead, drizzle a little of the oil onto roasted or steamed vegetables, use it to make a simple sauce for pasta, or stir into freshly cooked noodles just before serving. It can be used in small quantities, in place of some of the fat or oil in a recipe, to add flavor to cakes and cookies, especially those that contain walnuts.

Walnut oil does not keep for long and, after opening, should be kept in a cool, dark place to prevent it from becoming rancid. It can be stored in

Quick Ideas for Dressings and Salads

A good dressing should enhance rather than overpower the salad.

• To make a simple vinaigrette dressing, whisk together 4 tablespoons extra virgin olive oil with 1 tablespoon red or white wine vinegar or balsamic vinegar in a small pitcher. Add a pinch of sugar and 1 teaspoon Dijon mustard. Season to taste.

• To make a walnut oil dressing, whisk together 4 tablespoons walnut oil with 1 tablespoon sherry vinegar, then season to taste. This dressing is good with strong flavored leaves, such as arugula, watercress, or radicchio.

• Combine walnut oil and low-fat fromage frais or yogurt with chopped fresh flat leaf parsley. Season, then spoon the dressing over new potatoes, and garnish with snipped chives and toasted chopped walnuts.

• Mix together grated fresh ginger, fresh cilantro, lime juice, and toasted sesame oil and pour onto grated carrot. Sprinkle toasted sesame seeds on top of the carrot mixture.

• Mix together extra virgin olive oil and lemon juice, and spoon over warm flageolet and cannellini beans. Add chopped tomatoes and chopped fresh flat leaf parsley.

• Toss steamed broccoli flowerets or sugar snap peas in a dressing made from hazelnut oil, olive oil, white wine vinegar, and Dijon mustard.

the fridge, but this may cause it to solidify. Walnut oil is rich in polyunsaturated fats and contains vitamin E.

Hazelnut oil

This fine, fragrant oil is rich brown in color and has a delicious, roasted hazelnut flavor. It is quite expensive to buy but, because it has such a strong flavor, only a little is needed. It is good, combined with less strongly flavored oils, for salad dressings and sauces, and can be used to add a nutty flavor to sweet breads, cakes, cookies, and pastry. Hazelnut oil is rich in monounsaturated fat.

Almond oil

This pale, delicate oil is mainly used in confectionery and desserts. It has a subtle, sweet flavor of almonds, although it is not strong enough to give an almond flavor to baked goods, such as cakes and cookies. Almond oil is rich in monounsaturated fat as well as vitamins A and E. It is reputed to

Walnut, sesame, and hazelnut oils

be very good for the skin and is often used as a massage oil.

Buying and Storing: Cooking oils, such as sunflower, soy, and safflower, are more stable than nut or seed oils, and have longer keeping properties. To keep them at their peak, store in a cool, dark place away from direct sunlight. Nut and seed oils are more volatile and turn rancid quickly and should be kept in the fridge after opening.

Health Benefits: Oils are undeniably high in calories and should always be used in moderation, but they also have a number of health benefits. Monounsaturated fats, found particularly in olive oil and canola oil, either stabilize or raise the level of the beneficial high density lipoproteins (HDLs), while lowering harmful low density lipoproteins (LDLs), thus keeping down blood cholesterol levels in the body. A high level of LDLs in the blood is usually an indication of increased cholesterol levels, as the LDLs

carry the fatty substance (cholesterol) around the body; HDLs, however, carry much less fat.

Olive oil also contains vitamin E, a natural antioxidant that can help fight off free radicals, which damage cells in the body and have the potential to cause cancer. Polyunsaturated fats provide essential fatty acids known as omega-3 (alpha-linolenic) and omega-6 (linolenic acid), which must be included in the diet. Omega-3, which is found in walnut, canola, and soy oil, has been found to reduce the likelihood of heart disease and blood clots, while omega 6, provided by safflower, sunflower, and walnut oil, reduces harmful cholesterol levels. Polyunsaturated fats are more unstable than monounsaturated fats and are prone to oxidation, which can lead to the build-up of free radicals. Although polyunsaturates do contain vitamin E, it appears in varying amounts and so it is advisable to eat other foods that are rich in vitamin E to protect the fatty acids and the body from damage due to oxidation.

Vinegars

One of our oldest condiments, vinegar is made by acetic fermentation, a process that occurs when a liquid containing less than 18 percent alcohol is exposed to the air. Most countries produce their own type of vinegar, usually based on their most popular alcoholic drink—wine in France and Italy, sherry in Spain, rice wine in Asia, and beer and cider in Great Britain. Commonly used as a preservative in pickles and chutneys, it is also an ingredient in marinades and salad dressings. A spoonful or two of a good-quality vinegar can add flavor to cooked dishes and sauces.

WINE VINEGARS

These can be made from white, red, or rosé wine, and the quality of the vinegar will depend on the quality of the original ingredient. The finest wine vinegars are made by the slow and costly Orleans method. Cheaper and faster methods of fermentation involve heating, which produces a harsher vinegar that lacks the complexities of the original wine. Use in dressings, mayonnaise, sauces or to add flavor to stews and soups.

BALSAMIC VINEGAR

This is a rich, dark, mellow vinegar, which has become hugely popular. Made in Modena in northern Italy, balsamic vinegar

Sherry vinegar

is made from grape juice (predominantly from Trebbiano grapes), which is fermented in vast wooden barrels for a minimum of four to five years and up to 40 or more years, resulting in an intensely rich vinegar with a concentrated flavor. Balsamic vinegar is delicious in dressings or sprinkled over roasted vegetables. It is even good with strawberries.

SHERRY VINEGAR

This vinegar can be just as costly as balsamic vinegar and, if left to mature in wooden barrels, can be equally good. Sweet and mellow in flavor, sherry vinegar is caramel in color and can be used in the same way as balsamic vinegar—in dressings, sprinkled over roasted vegetables, or added to sauces and stews.

RASPBERRY VINEGAR

Any soft fruit can be used to enhance the flavor of white wine vinegar, but raspberries are the most popular. Raspberry vinegar can be made at home by macerating fresh raspberries in good-quality wine vinegar for 2–3 weeks. Once the mixture is strained, the vinegar is delicious as part of a salad dressing, or in sauces. It can be mixed with sparkling mineral water to make a refreshing drink.

MALT VINEGAR

Made from sour beer, malt vinegar is used in Britain and other northern European countries for pickling onions and other vegetables, or for sprinkling over french fries. It can be clear, but is often sold colored with caramel. Malt vinegar has a robust, harsh flavor and it is not suitable for salad dressings.

Balsamic vinegar

Red and white wine vinegars

Raspberry vinegar

RICE VINEGAR

There are two kinds of rice vinegar: the type from Japan is mellow and sweet and is most often used to flavor sushi rice, but it can also be added to dressings, stir-fries, and sauces; Chinese rice vinegar is much sharper in taste. Rice vinegar is usually a clear, pale brown color, but it can also be inky-black, red or white.

CIDER VINEGAR

Made from cider and praised for its health-giving properties, cider vinegar is made in the same way as wine vinegar. It is a clear, pale-brown color and has a slight apple flavor, but it is too strong and sharp to use in the same ways as wine vinegar. It can be used for salad dressings, but it is perhaps best kept for pickling fruits such as pears. Cider vinegar can be served as a soothing drink, mixed with honey, lemon juice, and hot water, as a remedy for colds and flu.

Health Benefits: Hippocrates prescribed vinegar as a cure for respiratory problems, and it may also be beneficial in cases of food poisoning. Cider vinegar is said to have many therapeutic benefits, which were highlighted in a book written in the 1960s by Dr DeForest Clinton Jarvis, entitled *Folk Medicine.* He attributed cider as a cure for everything, from arthritis and headaches, to obesity and hiccups.

Above: Cider vinegar

Fragrant Spiced Vinegar

This aromatic vinegar is good in dressings and marinades. Any type of vinegar can be used as a base but, to achieve the best results, ensure that it is good quality. If the vinegar develops an unpleasant appearance or aroma, it should be discarded straight away.

Different flavorings, including herb sprigs such as tarragon or rosemary, or whole spices such as cinnamon, star anise, or black, white, or green peppercorns can be used, and will impart a distinctive flavor.

1 Put a few red chile peppers, 1–2 garlic cloves, and some thick strips of lemon rind in a bottle of rice vinegar. Leave on a sunny window ledge or in a warm place for 3–4 weeks.

2 Strain the vinegar into a clean bottle and seal tightly with a cork. Store in a cool, dark place.

Rice vinegar (left) and brown malt vinegar

Teas & Tisanes

Tea has been a popular reviving drink for centuries and comes in many different forms, from traditional teas such as green tea, oolong tea, and black tea, to fragrant fruit infusions and healing herbal tisanes.

GREEN TEA

This tea is popular with the Chinese and Japanese who prefer its light, slightly bitter but nevertheless refreshing flavor. It is produced from leaves that are steamed and dried, but not fermented, a process that retains their green color.

OOLONG TEA

Partially fermented to produce a tea that falls between the green and black varieties in strength and color, oolong tea is particularly fragrant.

Black tea (left) and green tea

BLACK TEA

This is the most widely available tea and is made by fermenting withered tea leaves, then drying them. It produces a dark brown brew that has a more assertive taste than green tea. Darjeeling and English breakfast tea are two examples.

Health Benefits: The latest research shows that drinking about five cups of tea a day may help to prevent heart disease, stroke and certain cancers. These benefits have been attributed to a group of antioxidants found in tea, which are called polyphenols or flavonoids. Flavonoids have antiviral, antibacterial, and anti-inflammatory properties. Green tea contains the highest amount of flavonoids and black tea the lowest. Antioxidants help to mop up harmful free radicals, which cause damage to the body's cells and may cause cancer. Tea also contains fluoride, which can protect the teeth against decay. On the down side, tea can reduce the absorption of iron if drunk after a meal and it contains caffeine (although less than coffee), which is a well-known stimulant.

FRUIT TEAS

These are made from a blend of fruit flavors, such as rosehip, strawberry, orange, raspberry, and lemon, along with fruit pieces and sometimes herbs or real tea. It is a good idea to check the packaging to make sure the "tea" is naturally, rather than artificially, flavored. Fruit teas make refreshing caffeine-free drinks, which are almost calorie-free. They are an ideal drink for pregnant women and, because of their low-sugar content, are suitable for diabetics.

Oolong tea

Coffee

Although coffee is generally viewed as unhealthy, largely due to its high level of caffeine, studies have shown that it can enhance concentration and elevate mood. However, drinking more than six cups a day can increase the risk of heart disease and high blood pressure.

HERBAL TISANES

Although herbal tisanes are of little nutritional value, herbalists have prescribed them for centuries for a multitude of ailments and diseases. These teas (made from the leaves, seeds, and flowers of herbs) are a convenient and simple way of taking medicinal herbs. They do, however, vary in strength and effectiveness. Store-bought teas are generally mild in their medicinal properties, but are good, healthy, caffeine-free drinks. Even so, some varieties are not recommended for young children and pregnant women and so it is advisable to check the packaging. Teas that are prescribed by herbalists can be incredibly powerful and should be taken with care.

The most popular types of herbal teas are listed below.

Peppermint tea is recommended as a digestive to be drunk after a meal. It is also effective in settling other stomach problems and for treating colds. **Camomile tea** soothes and calms the nerves and can induce sleep. **Raspberry leaf tea** prepares the uterus for birth and is said to reduce labor pains, but it is not recommended in early pregnancy. It can also relieve period pains. **Rosehip tea** is high in Vitamin C and may help to ward off colds and flu. **Dandelion and lemon verbena** teas are effective diuretics. **Rosemary tea** can stimulate the brain and improve concentration. **Thyme tea** can boost the immune system and fight viral, bacterial, and fungal infections. **Elderflower** tea can ease painful sinuses and bronchial conditions.

Below: Naturally flavored fruit teas are caffeine-free and contain hardly any calories

Elderflower and dandelion herbal tisanes

Flavored Teas

These could not be easier to make: simply steep your chosen herb, spice, or fruit in boiling water and leave to infuse before straining. Ginger tea is effective against nausea, colds and flu, and stomach upsets.

1 To make ginger tea, roughly chop a 1-inch piece of fresh ginger root. Place in a cup and pour in boiling water.

2 Cover and leave for 7–10 minutes. Strain or drink as it is—the ginger will stay in the bottom of the cup.

Sweeteners

Nutritionists have wide-ranging—and often extreme—opinions on sugar and sugar alternatives. Some maintain that these products cause hyperactivity in children, while others believe that sugars can induce relaxation and sleep. Many recipes from breads and cakes to desserts and puddings contain different types of sugar and/or sugar substitutes, such as molasses, honey, malt, and grain syrups, as well as dried fruit, and wouldn't be palatable without them. So, as long as a diet is well-balanced and varied, it is considered that moderate amounts of sugar are nutritionally acceptable.

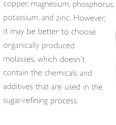

Black molasses

MOLASSES

This rich, syrupy liquid is a by-product of sugar refining and ranges in quality and color. The most nutritionally valuable type is thick and very dark blackstrap molasses, which contains less sugar than lighter alternatives and is richer in iron, calcium, copper, magnesium, phosphorus, potassium, and zinc. However, it may be better to choose organically produced molasses, which doesn't contain the chemicals and additives that are used in the sugar-refining process.

HONEY

One of the oldest sweeteners used by man, honey was highly valued by the ancient Egyptians for its medicinal and healing properties. The color, flavor, consistency, and quality of honey depends on the source of nectar as well as the method of production. In general the darker the color, the stronger the flavor. Many commercial brands of honey are pasteurized and blended to give a uniform taste and texture, but from the point of view of both flavor and health, it is best to buy raw unfiltered honey from a single flower source.

Nutritionally, honey offers negligible benefits, but as it is much sweeter than sugar, less is needed; it is also lower in calories. Today, honey still retains its reputation as an antiseptic, and recent studies show that it is effective in healing and disinfecting wounds if applied externally. Mixed with lemon and hot water, it can relieve sore throats and is also thought to be helpful in treating diarrhea and asthma.

Carob and carob powder

CAROB

This caffeine-free alternative to chocolate is made from the aromatic, fleshy bean of a Mediterranean tree. Carob flour

Honey

Malt extract

Dried fruit

looks and tastes similar to unsweetened cocoa and can be used to replace it in hot drinks, confectionery, and baked goods. It is naturally sweeter and lower in fat than unsweetened cocoa, as well as being more nutritious, providing iron, calcium, vitamin B$_6$, riboflavin, and potassium.

MAPLE SYRUP

This is made from the sap of the maple tree. Look for pure varieties rather than maple-flavored syrup, which contains additives. Maple syrup has a rich, distinctive flavor and is sweeter than sugar, so less is required in cooking.

GRAIN SYRUPS

Corn, barley, wheat, and rice can be transformed into syrups that are used in place of sugar in baked goods and sauces. Grain syrups tend to be easier to digest and enter the bloodstream more slowly than other forms of refined sugar, which cause swings in blood-

sugar levels. Grain syrups are not as sweet as sugar and have a mild, subtle flavor. Malt extract, a by-product of barley, has a more intense flavor and is good in breads and other baked goods.

FRUIT JUICE

Freshly squeezed fruit juice is a useful alternative to sugar in baked goods, sauces, pies, and ice cream. Fruit juice concentrates, such as apple, pear, and grape, which have no added sugar or preservatives, are available from health-food stores. They can be diluted or used in concentrated form in cakes, pies, and desserts.

Clockwise from left: Date syrup, barley malt syrup and brown rice syrup

DRIED FRUIT

Dates are made into a syrup with a rich flavor that can be used to sweeten cakes. Puréed dried fruits, such as prunes, figs, dates, and apricots, can replace sugar in pies and cakes. Dried fruit can be added to both sweet and non-sweet foods.

Spiced Apricot Purée

This richly spiced purée is delicious stirred into thick unsweetened yogurt or can be used to sweeten cakes, crumbles, and pies.

1 Place 1½ cups dried apricots in a saucepan with enough water to cover. Add 1 cinnamon stick, 2 cloves, and ½ teaspoon freshly grated nutmeg. Bring to a boil, then simmer for 20 minutes, until the apricots are plump.

2 Let cool, then process in a food processor until smooth. Add more water if the mixture seems a little thick.

Index

Author's Acknowledgements

For their help, patience and support, I'd like to give special thanks to Jo Younger, James Fisher and Fatima for their inspiring and delicious ideas and suggestions; and Linda Fraser for giving me the opportunity to write this book and for her continued support and guidance. Thanks, too, to Alan Long for his advice. Finally, special thanks to my husband Silvio for his everlasting patience, support. I would also like to acknowledge the following books and organizations that were helpful in my research: *Food Your Miracle Medicine*, Jean Carper, Simon & Schuster, 1993; *Delicatessen Food Handbook*, Glynn Christian, Macdonald and Co, 1982; *The Realeat Encyclopedia of Vegetarian Living*, Peter Cox, Bloomsbury 1994; *Sophie Grigson's Ingredients Book*, Mitchell Beazley, 1991; *Wholefoods Companion*, Dianne Onstad, Chelsea Green Publishing Co. US., 1996; *Foods That Harm, Foods That Heal*, Reader's Digest, 1996; *Healing Foods*, Miriam Polunin, Dorling Kindersley, 1997; *The Food Pharmacy*, Jean Carper, Simon & Schuster, 1989; Solgar Vitamins; Health and Diet Co., and Quest Vitamins.